Goddesses Don't
Wear Orange

Goddesses Don't Wear Orange

Laura Weber

Cover design by Chris DeFillippi
Book design by: Sue Balcer

ISBN paperback: 978-0-9996488-1-0
ISBN e-book: 978-0-9996488-0-3

FIRST EDITION

To my Dad from whom I received my love of writing.
And my curly hair.

CHAPTER 1

Breakups

Breakups are hard, and no one gets through them with dignity. You get through them by binge-eating pizza off a Frisbee in bed. By doing errands with mascara streaking down your cheeks. By showing up at your ex's house in a tattered wedding dress and burning his shit on the front lawn.

By surviving it.

But after the misery subsides you move forward. You get bangs, go out with your girlfriends, and stop eating peanut butter by the ladle. You get on with your life.

Unfortunately, what you're about to read isn't a story about resilient women who moved forward, who handled things well.

No.

This is a story of unhinged women imprisoned in the heart of Maine, near to nature and far from men. Women whose crimes turned warriors' loins to jelly and sparked a 75 percent jump in abstinence at local area high schools.

This is the story of Coffee Correctional Facility for Bitter and On-Edge Women.

CHAPTER 2

Maybe She's Born with It, Maybe It's Hysteria

Coffee was opened in the early fifties by a group of philandering politicians for the purpose of stowing away mistresses during election years. It's bad business for spurned lovers to come out of the woodwork, so they locked them up, away from the public eye.

As gag orders gained popularity, politicians no longer needed the facility to hide their dirty laundry. Therefore, they sold the complex off to prison reform advocates, who repurposed it into Maine's first (and only) "progressive rehabilitation" penitentiary for women—women like me. Florence. Prisoner 4557.

The concept was simple.

If we complied with intensive group therapy, individual therapy, and every other kind of hippy-dippy therapy, we could get out in as little as sixteen months. But if the Rehabilitation Board decided that we couldn't be fixed by the five-and-a-half-year mark, we would be sent to a traditional state penitentiary to serve out the remainder of our lengthy sentence.

I know what you're thinking: *Sixteen months for heinous crimes? The liberals have gone soft!*

Well, you can calm down, you fascist jerk. The system works. Prisoners released from Coffee have a reoffending rate of 5 percent. To put that in perspective, the next-lowest rate is held by Norway's prisons at 20 percent.

Now you might be thinking: *Coffee's numbers are impressive! Those liberals are onto something!*

Well, you can calm down, you socialist prick. Coffee's strict admittance guidelines have everything to do with its rehabilitative success. Coffee only accepts women who 1) have murdered or attempted to murder a "male with whom she was closely associated," 2) have no documented mental health diagnoses or substance dependencies, and 3) are "deemed to have a low rate of recidivism." And did I mention that the unfixable ones get shipped off? A monkey could open a prison with those guidelines and get the same numbers. But more on the Warden later.

The truth of it is, Coffee is just another way for investors to line their pockets with government money and for prison reformers to feel like they are doing something significant.

The public isn't complaining, though. Coffee is still rehabilitating the Menstrual Minority while simultaneously keeping the crazies out of the dating scene. And thank goodness for that, because no man wants to end up on a date with a woman who might, on a whim, cut off his penis. But then again, maybe you don't deserve a penis if you're going to be an idiot.

And *that* was the kind of shit I kept to myself as I sat obediently in group therapy, unsuccessfully trying to avert my eyes from the insidious bulge in Dr. Sean's one-size-too-small khakis.

"As this is our last group therapy session before the Rehabilitation Seminars, I want each of you to share one thing you've learned from our time together. It doesn't need to be lengthy, but I want you to tell us what you've gotten out of this."

My mind drifted from the peeling floral wallpaper to the coffee-stained carpet. This was my fourth "group therapy termination" since being at Coffee, and I wasn't interested in hearing people's self-actualizations. Yeah—you probably shouldn't have stabbed your husband seven times in the chest. That tends to make people dead.

"Florence." Dr. Sean waved his arms in the air. "Stay with us. Will you please share what you've gotten out of our group time?"

I cleared my throat. "I learned it's important to communicate honestly." It was a somewhat inspired variation of what I said every year.

"Very good." He smiled, revealing the slight gap between his front teeth. "From what I have seen, you are learning what it means to be a functional woman in a healthy relationship."

Oh sweet baby angel. How badly you want us to stop carving shanks out of yogurt cartons and reintegrate into society!

"My turn?" First Lady Abigail squeaked.

"Yes, Abigail."

"I've learned that it was the hurt inflicted by my parents' inattentiveness that manifested itself in my abusive behavior toward men."

"Wonderful," Dr. Sean cooed.

Blaming the parents was always a safe bet. It's not your fault that the sugary cereal they gave you stunted the growth of your prefrontal cortex. There are books out there to prevent that kind of thing. Get a Kindle, Mom and Dad!

"Jessica?"

Crazy Jessie ruffled her curly hair. "I'm not apologizing. He deserved what he got. Lying bastard."

With a heavy sigh, Dr. Sean scribbled in his tattered notebook. Many inmates were unaware of the power that this seemingly innocuous man had over them. The Rehabilitation Board treated his assessments as holy gospel, and if he wasn't convinced you were rehabilitated, neither were they.

"Becky?" he pressed on.

"The breathing and counting exercises you taught us were good. They help me take a step back."

Admittedly, most of the women had gotten something out of therapy, but I had milked the therapy cow dry. Its udders were chapped and sore, and if I tried to get more out of it, I was going to get a swift hoof to the boob. There are only so many times you can talk about the highs and lows of your week. My eyelids grew heavy at the thought.

"Florence," Dr. Sean called out. "We're almost done."

I rubbed my eyes.

"Lorraine, your turn."

"What have I discovered in our time together . . ." Feminist Lorraine clicked her tongue against the roof of her mouth. "How about that our patriarchal culture punishes women because we dare to take action against men?"

"Lorraine, I hope you have gleaned more from our time than that. There are men, like me, who'd like to see you succeed." She opened her mouth to dispute that, but he quickly moved on. "Last, but certainly not least: Yvette."

"I've learned that you are incredibly sexy." Nympho Yvette, a heavily tattooed woman weighing in at approximately one Olsen twin, winked at the good doctor.

"While I appreciate the compliment, it's inappropriate." Dr. Sean turned his attention back to the group. "All right. For those of you who don't know, the Rehabilitation Board meets tonight. They'll review how far you've progressed in the last year and decide which of you will proceed onto the last leg of your journey here: the Rehabilitation Seminars. If you qualify, at eight o'clock tomorrow evening, a guard will escort you to the conference room, and you'll be fully briefed on what will be expected of you during the Seminars." He looked around, meeting each woman's gaze in turn. "I have genuinely enjoyed seeing your growth through this process, and if you don't advance to the Rehabilitation Seminars, it just means you have a little more growing to do. Have a good afternoon, ladies."

CHAPTER 3

The Feminist Mystique

In groups of three, we were escorted to private rooms for "positive social interaction without male supervision." We were free to talk about periods, rainbows, C-sections, glitter, anything we wanted! Except that we were monitored through cameras, just to make sure we didn't strangle each other with our hair.

There were ten positive interaction rooms at Coffee, and they all looked alike. One of the walls had a giant blackboard, which we were encouraged to express ourselves on. The other wall was lined with long shelves loaded with board games, books, and children's toys. It looked a lot like my old Sunday school classroom, but instead of a long, stubby table for mini-disciples, there were mismatched couches, love seats, and decrepit beanbag chairs.

"That took for-ev-er." Nympho Yvette dramatically collapsed into a purple armchair. "Never again."

"Don't get your hopes up," I said. "You're only in your first year. Most people have to do a second round before the Board approves them."

"Oh, Florence." She threw her hands over her heart. "You're a shining beacon of hope in this dark, dark world."

I grinned. "Hey, I'm just warning you."

Feminist Lorraine stared off into the distance, biting a hang-nail. "Am I the only one who notices how sexist Dr. Sean is?"

"Yep, you're full of shit."

"Go fuck yourself, Florence. You know, if you'd read any-thing about the women's liberation movement, it'd be obvious to you that—"

Gosh, I loved that feminist psycho—full of fervor and lady venom. To the untrained eye, she might appear an incorri-gible political crusader, but to really grasp the entirety of who Feminist Lorraine was, one needed to step back in time.

Little Lorraine was born in a small town somewhere east of the Mississippi. Her father: a butcher. Her mother: a nurse.

One night, thanks to a forward-thinking schoolteacher, Little Lorraine got her hands on *The Feminine Mystique*. When Zeus's masculine bolt smote her not upon touching the book, she devoured it cover to cover. And thus Little Lorraine was gone, and Feminist Lorraine was born.

Like any good picket-toting feminist, she went to rallies, refused deodorant, and dated a series of neurotic social activ-ists. Eventually, she settled down and began a catering business. Before long, she was recruited to host one of the most presti-gious feminist banquets in the United States.

On the day of the banquet, amidst the chaos of centerpiec-es and vulva-shaped ice sculptures, a wrinkled old man from her hometown came to visit her. To the casual observer, this elderly man might have seemed precious, what with his cane and slightly hunched back. But he wasn't precious; he was a vile man, a predator with a predilection for little girls, a predator who used to babysit Little Lorraine when her parents went to Friday night bingo.

God knows why he sought her out after all those years. Maybe he thought she had forgotten his sins and that bygones were bygones. If so, he was wrong. He would have been safer trying to infiltrate ISIS in a Captain America suit.

Nonetheless, he said hello.

If that had been it, if he had left after that (with haste!), he might have lived to tell about it. But he, like all vile men, couldn't help himself. He reached out to graze her soft cheek one last time, and before his familiar, wrinkled hands could touch her again, Feminist Lorraine struck back.

That night, Feminist Lorraine received compliment upon compliment, until word got out about what made the appetizers so decedent.

How you say . . . *les pommes des hommes*? *Les testicles*?

A shocked silence fell upon the room, followed by the sound of a hundred men and women dry heaving. (And wet heaving. Is that a word? I wet heave, you wet heave, he/she/it wet heaves?) Hence, Feminist Lorraine's eventual arrival at Coffee.

Back to our scheduled rant.

"—And like Betty Friedan said, 'No woman gets an orgasm from shining the kitchen floor!'"

"She must not be doing it right," Nympho Yvette replied with a wolfish smile.

"You're my kind of woman, Yvette," Feminist Lorraine stated with a hint of admiration. "You embrace your sexual agency without reservation!"

"Sexual agency?"

"It means you sleep with whomever you want, whenever you want, in whatever position you want. On *your* terms."

"Huh, it sounds like a good thing, but it also sounds like you're calling me a slut."

"Ha!" I blurted.

"Hey, I am very particular about who I bang! My vagina is a locked house, and only guys who have the key can get in." Nympho Yvette smirked impishly. "It just so happens that a circumcised penis is the skeleton key."

A voice blared overhead. "So most men in the Western hemisphere have access to your special lady-house?"

Ten seconds later, a key turned in the lock, and a curly-haired goon stuck his head into the room. "Did you guys know there's an intercom for these rooms? So cool."

Greg stepped into the doorway, broom in hand, looking as gangly as the day I met him. His Northern Wisconsin drawl, coupled with his awkward demeanor, made him just socially backward and asexual enough for us to become close friends. "I was napping in the monitor room when Yvette woke me up with all her vagina-house talk."

"The guards don't care if you crash in there?" Feminist Lorraine asked.

"No, they're too busy showing off pictures of their grandkids."

"And yet women work twice as hard, and get paid seventy cents on the dollar..."

I ignored her. "Shouldn't you be cleaning the Warden's office? You know, instead of sleeping?"

"No way. The Warden's office is cursed. Squirrels keep sneaking in there and dying. It's a straight-up graveyard in there."

I rolled my eyes. "His office isn't cursed. It's whatever that chemical plant next door is pumping out. Must be bad for the squirrels. This happens every June."

"Summer is truly a magical time in this hellhole." He shook his head. "How was the last group session with Dr. S.?"

"Fine," I muttered, playing with the orange frays of the couch cushion.

"I have a good feeling this time, Flo," Greg said. "I think they're going to choose you for the Seminars."

"We'll see."

Nympho Yvette snorted. "As you know, Greg, Florence doesn't believe in hope or optimism or any good things happening at all."

"I don't blame her," Feminist Lorraine stretched her arms above her head. "If she doesn't get chosen tomorrow, she's going to prison for the rest of her life."

"Shut up!" Greg's curly eyebrows furrowed. "Don't listen to her, Flo."

I shrugged. She wasn't wrong. This was my fifth year at Coffee. If the Rehabilitation Board thought I was still a danger to society, I was going away for a long time. I tried not to think about it.

Nympho Yvette rolled out of her chair, landing in front of the giant blackboard. "Since no one knows what the Seminars are, I wanna hear your theories." She picked up a piece of chalk. "Who's first?"

"I think they're going to make you watch *Dr. Phil* for a year straight." Greg leaned on his broom.

She scribbled *Dr. Phil* on the board. "Next?"

"I hope it's some sort of challenge," Feminist Lorraine said. "Like *American Ninja Warrior*."

American Ninja Warrior went up.

"I hope it's a challenge like not fantasizing about Dr. Sean." Nympho Yvette drew a rough sketch of Dr. Sean in a gladiator outfit and ran her tongue along her front teeth. "I want to use him like a hand mirror. Do my makeup in his bald spot."

"And that's my cue," Greg said. "See you for laundry duty?"

I gave him a lazy two-finger salute. "Aye, aye, Captain."

He flashed a lopsided smile and disappeared out the door.

"GET A ROOM!" Nympho Yvette hollered. "Take him to the conjugal trailer already. Give him all the herpes!"[1]

"Please, he's like a golden retriever. He's fun and loyal, but getting intimate with a golden retriever is bestiality. And bestiality is illegal. So essentially, being with Greg would be illegal."

"It's incredible how much you like him." Nympho Yvette circled her hands around her mouth and bellowed in my ear, "Florence and Greg, sitting in a tree, h-u-m-p-i-n-g!"

"God, Yvette, don't be dumb," Feminist Lorraine said. "She doesn't like Greg."

"Thank you!"

"Yeah, no, she's IN LOVE with Greg and is going to have his weird curly-haired babies."

I clapped my hands over my ears, attempting to block out the horrid mental image. "I hate you guys so much."

Someday, I told myself, I'd look back on this moment and laugh. And that day would be my wedding day. When Greg saw me in my wedding dress. From the audience. As I married James Franco.

---

1 Once located beside the west wing of the prison, the Conjugal Trailer was closed down two years ago after a crabs outbreak. I did my best not to think about that dark time in our pubes' lives.

CHAPTER 4

The Coffee Beans

At five the next morning, I woke up to the sound of raucous Irish women conjuring up grits and rehydrated eggs in the basement kitchen. Their Celtic jokes and loud laughter reverberated through the vents. After four and a half years, it was a homey comfort of sorts.

A few minutes later, the monotonous echo of a guard's footsteps began from afar. First round of the day—two hours until wake-up call.

By the slow pace of the steps, I could tell it was Officer Lenny. Soft-spoken Officer Lenny, who treated us kindly and fell asleep if he sat too long in the warm laundry room. As he patrolled each cell, I pictured the sleepers within.

Cell A: Feminist Lorraine.

Cell B: Nympho Yvette. She was the most sexually unrestrained nursing home aide this side of the Mason-Dixon. Her lady parts stopped the hearts of three elderly men in the span of two months.

Cell C: Crazy Jessie. She stabbed her ex-boyfriend with a chunk of iron rebar during a lightning storm. He was dead until lightning struck the rod, resuscitating him. Strategically, he visits every year right before the Rehabilitation Board meets. This consistently results in foaming-mouth threats of burning down his house, and another year for good ol' Crazy J.

Cell D: First Lady Abigail. She stalked a former president whose name she cannot legally disclose (but she said that he was white so, you know, that narrows it down). On his birthday, she surprised him, giving him a heart attack, which he survived. Granted, it was an accident, but given time, she would have skinned him alive and made a human Snuggie out of him.

Cell E: Lovely Elizabeth. She was a modest Brit who enjoyed listening to classical music and perfecting her croissant recipe. Even her crime read like a Charlotte Brontë novel . . .

Upon learning of her husband's cockfoolery, she prepared him a tainted soufflé. No one would have suspected her, had they not stumbled upon her garden fraught with carrots, tomatoes, spinach, thyme, and hemlock.

This girl was so classy that she used fucking hemlock to kill her husband.

Cell F: Gretchen. She dropped large-boned puppies off a high-rise YMCA, killing both the puppies and her ex-husband, who was standing on the sidewalk below. None of us were sure how someone so unhinged could possibly be eligible for Coffee, but our working theory was that her family was well connected and pulled some strings to circumvent the real prison system.

Lenny's footsteps grew louder, then faded as he sluggishly passed by my cell.

He shuffled on, checking on the Domestics (who all killed their husbands), Hot-Rod Kim (who cut her boyfriend's car brakes), and Susie the Strangler.

Four years ago, in the middle of the night, Susie the Strangler woke up thinking she'd heard something downstairs. Assuming that she had left the kitchen window cracked open, she went downstairs to close it . . . and came face to face with some white, middle-aged career criminal. The burglar slapped her, and a fistfight ensued. It ended with her strangling him. The DA argued that Susie the Strangler used excessive force and should've stopped strangling him once he was passed out. (Because apparently civilians are supposed to know the magic moment between passed out and dead.) Even though the burglar was not a "male with whom she was closely associated," the courts took it easy on her and sentenced her to Coffee.

Following Susie the Strangler was Becky Bear (who trained a grizzly bear to tear apart her husband), Yosemite Karen (who used her boyfriend as target practice), and Caroline/Carolyn/Coraline (who hooked her fiancé's junk to a dog's shock collar).

The rest of the cells were downstairs in the teen pregnancy ward.

Okay, fiiiiine. I didn't know for sure that there was a pregnancy ward down there, but it was an educated guess. Every once in a blue moon, we saw a pregnant girl or two in an prison uniform scurrying by, and no one would tell us who they were or where they came from. Except for Greg.

Greg claimed that the pregnant girls were daughters of Coffee's trustees who were being sequestered from the public eye to make weapons parts for military contractors. He even claimed that he had seen a signed military contract on the Warden's desk. Whether Greg was trying to feed the intrigue or was actually telling the truth, I wasn't sure. But I wouldn't put it past the Warden to take money from the military complex while the prison reformers lifted him on their shoulders as the patron saint of justice.

I slipped back into sleep, dreaming of pregnant girls manning machine guns until Officer Lenny lifted me out of sleep with a tender, "Flo, Flo, Flo your boat, gently down the stream."

CHAPTER 5

Dumbass

Apart from Gretchen incessantly slurping eggs off her plastic tray, breakfast proceeded in reverent silence. The air, normally laden with the chemicals from the processing plant next door, was now teeming with anticipation as well.

The dryers in the laundry room were just starting to heat up when Greg stopped in to say hello. Due to his harmless demeanor and general likability, the guards always allowed him a few minutes of chitchat before grunting suggestively for him to move along.

"Maybe the Seminars will be in a pool, and they'll waterboard you." To demonstrate, he put a dirty rag from his pocket over his face and began to flail.

I fed the washing machine linen treats. "I'm not doing this."

"Maybe," one of the Domestics cheerily chimed in, "they'll make us wear burlap sacks and beat us until we repent."

"Sounds like my husband!" The second member of the trio roared with laughter.

The third Domestic smacked her friend's sizable rear end. "You know it!"

Dr. Sean assured us in therapy that the Domestics' seemingly dark senses of humor about their abusive pasts were the "catalysts through which they transitioned from victims to survivors," but I figured they were just sociopaths who lied about domestic violence to get lighter sentences.

"Maybe . . ." Becky Bear eagerly tucked her short brown hair behind her ears. "Maybe they'll strand us in the middle of the desert and see who survives. We'll have to eat cactus and build shelters out of tumbleweeds!"

"They should chuck eggs at you so you know how it feels, you ovulating criminals!" Greg melodramatically threw himself against a dryer.

Feminist Lorraine glared at him. "Are you implying that when we committed our crimes, we metaphorically fired eggs out of our ovaries?"

"When the shoe fits."

"Take it off and beat you with it?" I suggested.

"That's the spirit of rehabilitation," he said, tapping me between the eyes. The guard on duty cleared his throat: Greg's hint to leave. "The next time I see you, you will know what your punishment shall be. Hung by your toes in the dungeon, methinks!"

After laundry duty, I sat listlessly in my cell, watching the clock. And as clock-watching goes, the day crawled by slowly and painfully. Once the big hand touched the twelve and the little hand touched the eight, I could give up hope. No guard would come to escort me, and I could resign myself to a future behind bars. Until then, hours and minutes danced together in a cruel fashion, thrashing against my skin, making it crawl.

My little slice of heaven felt even more claustrophobic than usual. It was your standard eight-by-eight jail cell with a single bed, toilet, and sink. Its only amenities were an unbreakable stainless steel mirror, a clock bolted to the wall, and a small TV suspended in upper corner of the cell. The TV was from the mid-nineties and only received six channels,[2] but beggars can't be choosers. We were allowed to decorate our walls with pictures, posters, and drawings. I'd decorated mine with torn-out *National Geographic* photos, which I changed each month when a new edition came in. Which was convenient, because the guards made us tear down our décor monthly to make sure we weren't burrowing through the walls to freedom.

I sat against the cold cinderblock wall, trying to straighten my misshapen spine. Unfortunately, my core was a memory foam pillow, so I ended up slumped on the ground. It's a myth that people who go to prison get in shape. Even with no Netflix, no dating, no snacks, and no way out, one can still find reasons not to work out. The human condition is impressive, both in its perseverance and in its ability to avoid treadmills.

I shut my eyes and listened to the tick of the clock. Gradually, the ticking disappeared, and I dreamt myself into a familiar blue room with chipping white trim. The fan spun quietly as I snuggled under the gray down comforter and turned sleepily to

---

2 Only three of which were in English.

the man beside me. His familiar smell filled my lungs, leaving behind sweet warmth. He never wore cologne, but he always smelled just a little bit like vanilla. I savored the up and down of his chest— the beautifully consistent rhythm that lulled me to sleep so many nights. I reached out to touch his side. I always loved his stomach and familiar proportions.

The loud pounding of a nightstick against cell bars yanked me out of our bed and back to my cold cell floor. I wanted to close my eyes to catch another glimpse of him, but I stopped myself. He was gone and so was that life. I shoved the memory to the back of my mind in the hope that a brain tumor would eat it.

"Thanks for joining us."

Still half asleep, I rose to greet the guards. "Officer Carmel, Officer Ramsey."

Coffee's guards were harmless; just lazy corrections officers looking to coast into retirement. Except for Ramsey and Carmel.

Ramsey was a power-hungry brute who relished being a big fish in a small pond. He often threatened violence, but most prisoners thought he was full of hot air. I knew better. In my first year, an inmate named Ashley yelled something horrible at him, and he took her to "cool off" outside. The next day in the shower, she had bruises all over her stomach. She claimed that she fell down the stairs, but I've never seen stairs shaped like fists.

Carmel, on the other hand, was the resident pervert. He'd graduated from the Academy last year and immediately come to Coffee. Since then, he had been undressing us with his beady eyes, making inappropriate comments, and propositioning us. He had yet to sleep with an inmate (as far as I knew), but he was getting there.

"You look tired, Florence," Officer Carmel said, smiling like a Cheshire cat. "Maybe I can take you to the supply closet and wake you up."

"Not now," Officer Ramsey grunted. "We've got to go."

"Fine." Officer Carmel grabbed the ring of keys around his belt. "You'd think the state could afford to give us swipe cards like hotels use. It's the freaking dark ages here."

"This isn't a Holiday Inn, rookie. If you have a problem with it, transfer."

"I'm not saying that. I'm just saying it'd make things easier—" He fumbled with his keys.

"Here." Officer Ramsey seized the keys. In two seconds, he unlocked my cell and shoved the keys back in Officer Carmel's hand. "Get the dumbass to the conference room."

My sleepy mind unsuccessfully tried to process their words. Dumbass . . . conference room . . . Then it hit me. THE CONFERENCE ROOM. The Rehabilitation Board picked me. ME! I WAS THE DUMBASS! My heart danced in my chest as they walked me down the hall.

The Conference Room, used for pole dancing class and Bible study, was vacant save for a small circle of chairs at the center. Feminist Lorraine, Lovely Elizabeth, and Susie the Strangler were already seated next to Dr. Sean. Officer Lenny returned with Yosemite Karen, and to my surprise, Officer Ramsey brought in Nympho Yvette. I guess they figured one year was sufficient for her to be rehabilitated. With that, all the chairs were filled. We were the Chosen. It wasn't until the door shut that I noticed the Warden standing in front of the room.

Hm, how does one describe the Warden? Start by farting into your hand and holding it over your face. No, no—that's immature. I'm better than that. The Warden was a dumb-as-a-rock whale carcass who hated us almost as much as we hated him.

According to the prison archives, the Warden had worked in the correctional system since he was eighteen, primarily in the Midwest. He hopped between prisons, accumulating civil rights violation charges along the way. By the time they were about to force him out of the field entirely, he was on his fourteenth. But apparently, number fourteen was the charm, and the Warden saw the error of his ways. Because that's when he started advocating for prisoners' rights in Chicago and rubbing elbows with influential human rights lawyers and politicians, greasing his way into their good graces. He spoke publicly and passionately about the prison system, its flaws, and how he had become victim to the institutional mindset.

Lies. All lies.

But it didn't matter. He became the poster boy of prison reform, and a year later, he was appointed warden of the progressive incarceration experience known as Coffee.

The Warden's pudgy fingers clutched a pile of papers. "I will be passing out syllabuses—"

"Syllabi," Yosemite Karen corrected.

"Excuse me?"

"It's syllabi, not syllabuses."

"You're out," he said in an even tone.

Yosemite Karen looked up at him in disbelief. "What?"

"You're done. Good luck next year. Officer Lenny, escort her back to her cell."

Yosemite Karen muttered profanities under her breath as Officer Lenny took her back to her cell. She wasn't the only one who was upset; I could see Dr. Sean grinding his teeth. He clearly didn't see correcting the Warden as a reason for dismissal, but he just as clearly wasn't going to say anything. How did I know this? Because he never stood up to the Warden. He just kept his head down and his mouth shut and wore away his enamel instead.[3]

"As I was saying, these syllabuses outline what your next year at Coffee will look like. Dr. Sean will brief you on the specifics of the Seminars."

Dr. Sean stood up tall for the Warden. He stretched his jaw (his post-grinding-teeth ritual), refocusing on the task at

---

3 For a therapist, he repressed a lot.

hand. "Well, this is quite an exciting time, isn't it? The five of you in this room were selected because we believe you have the potential to amalgamate into what we in the social sciences call 'society.'

"Now, 'society' is made up of all types of women"—*temptresses*—"but disruptive women"—*psycho bitches*—"degrade the very core of that 'society.' So in order to see if your time here has really rehabilitated you"—*calmed you the fuck down*—"you will be having monitored one-on-one interactions with men"—*wait . . .* —"to see if you can treat them well"—*hold on . . .* —"and equally as important, if you can allow them to treat you well." *Wait a second . . .*

Lovely Elizabeth spoke first. "Blind dates?"

NO.

"We prefer to call them Rehabilitation Seminars. Or Decaffeination."

CHAPTER 6

The Sperm Is Strong with These Ones

I didn't know whether to laugh at the absurdity of dating state-appointed lemmings or to cry because I hadn't eaten dinner and I was really hungry.

How had we not heard about this? At least fifteen years of respectable ex-cons before us, and no one bothered giving us a heads up?

What happened to solidarity? To synchronizing?

Nympho Yvette jumped in diplomatically. "Will the prophylactics be compliments of Coffee or will our dates be bringing them?"

"Sexual intercourse with any of the volunteers will result in expulsion from the program." The Warden's voice snapped like a whip.

"Unless they are attractive?"

Susie the Strangler chuckled. "Especially if they are attractive."

"So if they're ugly . . ."

"The ugly ones get you pregnant," I said. "They're so rarely laid that their sperm have time to bulk up, strengthen their tails."

"The Seminars," the Warden shouted over us, "will be held in a restaurant called The Open Door. For those of you who are not familiar with this establishment, it is a surprisingly nice restaurant located in Bangor, Maine. Yes, we are taking you to a real city, not a Podunk town. This isn't some greasy spoon—you are to take this seriously. The Open Door has agreed to host you people, and we will be securing it with minimal manpower. There will be two guards—"

"Times must be tough," Nympho Yvette murmured.

"Who," the Warden continued on, louder, "will tase you at the first sign of violence and will shoot you at the second. Being around men who are not Coffee personnel may trigger past behaviors. We are prepared for such an event."

"But we are confident that everything will go smoothly!" Dr. Sean piped in reassuringly.

"All your conversations will be private, but not confidential. We will not know what you talk about, but these men are not your lawyers. They are not your doctors. They are not your priests. The men will be given surveys at the end of each Seminar, which will contribute to the Rehabilitation Board's final decision as to whether or not you are fit to be released."

"Also," Dr. Sean added, "you will no longer need to participate in traditional group therapy, and you will only attend individual therapy on an as-needed basis. Consider this a test run for the real world. However, you will continue to participate in the other therapies offered."

"And you are still mandated to do chores. You will continue to do whatever chores are assigned to you." The Warden counted off on his fat, clubbed fingers. "Laundry duty, cleaning the cells, picking vegetables in the greenhouses, and any other shit we want you to do. Insubordination will not be tolerated!"

"But we have confidence that you will continue doing a terrific job as always!" Dr. Sean said enthusiastically.

The Warden rolled his eyes. "You will be supplied with clothing from the nearest Salvation Army, which will be delivered to your cell the day of the Seminar. I will not tolerate any whining about not liking the color or it not fitting right. You're not Cinderella and this isn't the ball. You get what you get." He inhaled quickly and continued. "Each of you will be assigned a day of the week. There will be no overlap. You will not see each other. It's rolling admission for volunteers, but that does not mean that you can get your boyfriends to sign up for your day of the week. Cronyism is taken very seriously, and background checks are thorough. If you try to pull the wool over our eyes, we will catch you. Lastly, let me be clear, you WILL NOT share any detail of Decaffeination with any inmate outside of the program. We cannot have anyone preparing to manipulate the system. If we find you in violation of this order, you will immediately be sent to a traditional facility to serve out your bid."

For the next thirty-two minutes, Dr. Sean took the lead, briefing us on the expectations of behavior, and warning us against off-putting conversation pieces such as politics, religion, and "would you rather" scenarios.

I was both surprised and bummed by the latter. Those were some of my best conversation starters! But Dr. Sean claimed that "would you rather" games often devolve quickly.

Valid point.

I've seen it start innocently enough: "Would you rather have x-ray vision or fly?" Then I've seen it get a skosh darker: "Would you rather be in a wheelchair or be blind?" Then, given enough time, I've seen it end in: *"NO! YOU CAN'T 'PASS!' YOU HAVE TO CHOOSE! WOULD YOU RATHER HAVE SEX WITH YOUR BROTHER OR MURDER YOUR GRANDMOTHER! PICK NOW!"*

Probably best to stay away from that if we wanted to get released, and not transferred to Shutter Island.

CHAPTER 7

Cat's out of the Bag

"Congratulations, girlfriend!" Greg gave me a hard high-five through my cell door, leaving my hand burning like a UTI. "Told ya you'd get in!"

"You called it."

"So what are the Seminars? Should I get some eggs?" He tried to play it off, but Greg wanted to know about the Seminars as badly as any prisoner. He was too low on the totem pole to be let in on Coffee's secrets.

I hesitated. "I can't tell you."

"Right." Greg winked.

I stayed silent. If telling anyone outside the program meant being kicked out, I wasn't going to risk it.

"Wait, are you serious?"

"I'm not allowed."

"You aren't *allowed*? What are you? Four?"

"Sssshhhh," I warned.

"If you don't tell me, I'm going to pee into your cell." He threateningly unzipped the top of his blue jumpsuit.

"Be. Cool." I peeked at the guard at the end of the hall, but he was busy reprimanding Gretchen for trying to bite him.

So I motioned Greg to come closer. I knew telling him was a risk, and if anyone found out, I'd be spending the next twenty-five to life in prison. But if there was one thing I was sure about, it was that Greg wouldn't purposely hurt me. For all his flaws, he cared about me. So, I spilled the beans.

Greg stood dumbstruck. "That. Is. Hilarious."

"Shut up."

"They call it Decaffeination." He chuckled. "That's so lame."

"The Warden probably came up with it and decided it was the cleverest thought he's ever had." I paused, considering this. "It probably *was* the cleverest thought he's ever had."

"Yeah, he's an idiot." Greg chuckled again. "Decaffeination. That's emotional torture. You'll have to sit there, talk about their pointless days and careers . . ."

I felt a pang in my chest. Part of me missed sharing my pointless days with someone.

"Who's going to date prisoners anyways? Other prisoners?"

"No," I said. "They're supposedly volunteers from the community."

"Well, enjoy that top-notch company!" He laughed. "I guess after all this practice you'll be a pro at dating. Which is good, because after you get out, I'm taking you to dinner."

"All right, I'm always up for dinner with a friend."

Greg looked slightly deflated by my dropping the f-word. "Yeah, well, no Thai food."

"You fickle bastard." I glared.

He smirked. "And no Korean BBQ."

"I hate you."

"Love you. It's a date."

CHAPTER 8

I Believe in a Thing Called Love(less Marriage)

Everyone has a Greg: the absolute love of your life. Oh sorry, I meant the most friend-zoned person in your life. The kind of guy you pull pranks with, goof on movies with, and play tennis with. He's great, but the idea of kissing him makes you dry heave. That's Greg.

I wished it were different, but there wasn't any chemistry between us. I knew how obnoxiously vague that sounded, but it was the best I could do. It wasn't that Greg was unattractive or boring. My mom liked him, and my dad even tolerated him (better than I can say for my ex). For all intents and purposes, I should have jumped on the Greg bandwagon, but for whatever reason I couldn't. The chemistry, the "umph," the whatever you call it just wasn't there.

Then again, what did I know about love? I was deliriously happy with a prick. He was all the things I thought I wanted: smart, motivated, introspective. But for all his redeeming traits, fidelity wasn't one of them.

Ugh, I used to be such gullible romantic. I should've seen it coming. Even a cross-eyed deer can see the headlights before the car annihilates it. Maybe I *would* be better off in an arranged marriage with Greg, but I wasn't ready to give up the ship. Not yet, at least.

Nonetheless, Greg was a viable option for an arranged marriage. He had many attributes that would make him a fine arranged husband.

1. His presence was mostly pleasant.

2. Our kids would be well educated about the prison system.

3. He was taller than me, therefore able to reach high cupboards and clean ceiling fans.

If my adolescent self could see me weighing the pros and cons of marrying a prison janitor, I wouldn't have quit piano.

Sigh. *Oh, the illusion of youth.*

When I was young, pure and flat as unleavened bread, I was charming and unhindered. Once the lumps, humps, and curves emerged, I hid behind bulky sweatshirts and mom jeans. But even with my castration-inducing wardrobe, I caught my ex's eye. I was reading at my favorite café when he came up to me and, with sparkling eyes, asked if he could join me.

How much better it would have been if our initial eye contact had been interrupted by the gleam of a wedding ring! A sure sign his heart was for another! But no such glint caught my eye.

So we lingered. I heard his laugh before I heard his name, and two years later, we had a home we called our own.

Nope. Not anymore. Instead, I had a bright platonic future with a kid who couldn't pronounce the word "bagel."

Yep, I was doing just fine.

CHAPTER 9

Charlie Gibson

Nympho Yvette and I hung back against the courtyard wall, scoping out our kingdom in the early summer sun. Hot-Rod Kim ran around the yard, hair bouncing beautifully with each stride, her ass like two half cantaloupes that God himself had sliced and placed side by side.

Nympho Yvette lit her cigarette. "If there's ever an apocalyptic war that limits the number of men in this world, Kim's the first to die. Our bloodlines depend on it."

I nodded. "From your lips to Athena's ears."

The Domestics talked trash on the basketball court, while a couple others cheered them on. The more antisocial ones like First Lady Abigail, Crazy Jessie, and Caroline/Carolyn/Coraline sat on a picnic table talking spiritedly, while Gretchen crouched under said table, snacking on glue she'd lifted from art therapy. The excess dried into a winter frost on her mustache.

"It feels like absolute Shawshank in here." Susie the Strangler walked over, squinting her Southern eyes up at the Warden, who was watching us from his office. "Swear on my momma's grave, I'll never strangle anyone else as long as I live if it means never seein' that man again."

"And I'd give up sexing men to death." Then Nympho Yvette reconsidered. "It might be worth trying to sleep with the Warden first. If we're lucky, he's got a weak heart."

I suppressed a smile. I used to be shocked when the prisoners admitted to their crimes. I naively figured everyone would deny their guilt, but of all the prisoners, only one ever claimed to be innocent. She swore up and down that she didn't do it, but no one wanted to hear it. After a year, she realized it was pointless. Whining wasn't going to get her out any sooner, so she dropped it. Now she'd been here for nearly five years. But she had a great personality, an artistic spirit, soulful eyes—

FINE, YOU CAUGHT ME.

(*Takes off mask.*)

IT WAS ME!

Yes, it was true! I was innocent! And thus far, I had spent four and a half wrongfully imprisoned years surrounded by women who imaginatively murdered/attempted to murder the men in their lives. It took a long time for me to shut down my pity party. I wanted to feel sorry for myself, but then I realized it was pointless. All I could do was grin and bear it, which I couldn't have done it without the unexpected, strange camaraderie I found here.

We grieved and laughed with one another. We witnessed Greg unhinge his slightly slacked jaw and fit both his fists in his mouth. We watched the Warden receive awards for Nothingness: Doing Nothing Better Than Anyone Has Never Done Anything Before. We created this culture, a sub-society unto itself. I'd be lying if I said I'd never imagined a group of white coats observing us through a one-way mirror, jotting down notes about our bizarre shared lives.

But what we didn't share, what we barred one another from, was our lives Before Coffee (or BC). We shared stories of friends and family, but the relationships that landed us here were strictly off limits. There were moments, in therapy and mumbled sleep, where those portions of our lives came to light. Even then, the descriptions were fleeting, markedly vague and vaguely ominous.

. . . We were happy at first, but after seven years he lost his job and started hitting me.

. . . I thought I loved him, but one day I woke up and couldn't stand him.

. . . I felt powerless, but then I castrated him, ground up his testicles, and baked them into a mushroom and goat cheese quiche.

But in those first seven years, did he often volunteer to go to the store to buy milk so she didn't have to brave the gusty winter evening? Did she make him laugh with her fake German accent?

Before she snapped, did she love his family? Did they like her spirit? Did she blush when he told her so?

What was she like pre-testes pastry? What did she believe about the world?

What memories, once sweet, festered sourly in their stomachs?

My sour stomach came in waves, sometimes initiated by the most benign triggers. Once, I saw a dog on the news, and instantly, I was taken back to an urban pet store.

My ex and I had been dating for a month, and we were high on Early Relationship Spontaneity. We didn't live together and barely had enough money to go to the laundromat—but we didn't care. When you're that young and free, you don't worry about that sort of thing. You just throw it to the wind and buy a sixteen-year-old Great Dane with one eye and a wagging tail.

His name was Charlie Gibson, and he was the Leonardo DiCaprio of dogs. We took him to my apartment, got him an eye patch, and filled his last four months with walks, plush dog beds, and meaty on-the-bone dog treats. He went out a well-loved king.

But now, Charlie Gibson was blacklisted along with *The Wedding Singer*, sherbet-vanilla twist cones, April 14, Kierkegaard, and that douchey Wonderwall song.[4]

Dr. Sean told me that all good things become good again once we stop associating them with a painful memory. Maybe that was true. Maybe that day of healing would come, but until then, I felt like an emotional hemophiliac bound to be haunted by the things I used to love.

---

4   I really, truly, absolutely hate that song. "Oasis," you are the worst.

CHAPTER 10

Harrison

Preparing for the Seminars was a whirlwind of role-playing, proper silverware etiquette, and . . . wait for it . . . shaving our own legs! What a privilege! Normally, when we prisoners wanted our legs shaved, Coffee brought in an enormous broad-shouldered woman named Elda who wielded an antique straight razor. But not today! We were given safety razors and entrusted with maintaining our own hairy gams. It seemed our future reintegration into the outside world wasn't a pipe dream after all.

Another Decaf perk, unbeknownst to us, was that for our first Seminar, cosmetology students from the surrounding small towns were invited to practice on us. I dreaded looking like a Russian stacking doll, but after all was said and done, I was impressed with what I saw in the shatterproof mirror. I had two eyebrows now, after sporting a werewolf unibrow for years, and my chapped, pale lips were dark red and feminine like a dominatrix's. My cheeks even had a touch of blush, making them look warm. Per my request, my hair remained a brown, frizzy mess. I liked it that way. It made me feel feral and rebellious.

My outfit was a little less awe-inspiring, but it was still a nice change of pace from my bright orange prison onesie: black slacks and a short-sleeve green shirt. It wasn't fancy, but it was something.

And thus, it was time to party.

The Open Door was quaint: wood-paneled walls draped with oriental scarves caught the purples, blues, and greens ricocheting from the Turkish lamps. Soft music floated from hidden speakers, and savory smells from the kitchen wafted over me. Only a few couples sat amid the empty tables. Slow night.

All of a sudden, a breeze swept through the room, sending a devilish chill down my spine. My lover . . . he had arrived.

In slow motion, he handed a sheet of pink paper to Officer Ramsey, who nodded knowingly and motioned him to my table. As he neared, the light reflected off his form, transforming him for a moment into a knight in shining armor.

Unfortunately, the shining proved to be a nervous sweat, and his armor was flood pants with tighty-whities peeking out the top.

"I'm Florence," I said cordially.

"I'm Harrison," he replied nervously. "How are you?"

"I'm good. How are you?"

"Good." This was going swimmingly.

The waitress handed us menus and disappeared, leaving us to sit quietly for a tortuous five minutes and twenty-three seconds. After she returned and took our orders, we sat for an additional two minutes and fifteen seconds in total silence. I was going to have to force this conversation like a toddler into a beauty pageant.

"So Harrison, what do you do?"

"I am a chemical plant manager." He shifted in his seat. "At the plant next door to Coffee, actually. What do you do?"

"Well, I've been vacationing in a really quaint eight-by-eight villa as of late." I laughed to myself, then looked up to see Harrison wipe his nose awkwardly. *Damn it, Flo, can you not be sarcastic for one hour? Your freedom depends on it.*

"I'm sorry; I wasn't trying to be rude. I've been out of this scene for a while." Argh, why was I talking like a speed-dating divorcee? "Um, so yeah, before prison I was actually —"

"Hold on," he interrupted, "do my fingers smell weird to you? I smell bleu cheese but only near my finger pits." Before I had time to react, he shoved his fingers under my nose. "They smell, right?"

They did.

He continued to sniff his "finger pits" until the waitress returned with our food. Harrison's onion rings and clam chowder looked fine, but my meal was an utter masterpiece. Imagine two slices of warm ciabatta bread separated by thinly sliced prosciutto with pesto and sun-dried tomatoes—oh, the sundried tomatoes! Since being locked up, the closest thing I'd had to sun-dried tomatoes was a box of raisins Greg smuggled in for me. He ate half of them, and by the time he gave them to me, the box had collapsed, smashing all the raisins into a single colossal glob.

After Harrison's fingers had stopped smelling like cheese and started smelling like onion rings, he meandered back to the conversation. "So where did you work before prison?"

"Oh," I said, looking up from my sandwich, "a daycare."

And with that, the floodgates burst.

"A daycare?" He spoke speedily, but his words came out with almost robotic precision. "I can see that. You seem fairly maternal. Though isn't it still a cultural taboo to drop your kids off with strangers?" He took a quick breath and continued, "Did you know there is a hormonal reason that mothers can put up with so much crying and sleep deprivation?"

"Um, I think I heard—" I started.

"It's similar to—but different from—the hormonal reasons that the smell of our siblings repulses us enough to prevent attraction. Once I was at my sister's house, and across the street was an older couple that looked alike, but it wasn't because they were related, it was because when couples get older they tend to look like each other."

"Oh, yeah, my grandparents—"

"It's a strange phenomena really. Some people look like their dogs." He scraped chowder off his chin with his spoon. "I have owned five dogs in my life. That may seem like a lot, but it's not because I'm a bad dog owner. Quite the opposite, actually. I've always gotten older dogs."

Charlie Gibson flashed in my mind. "Me too."

"I think that says a lot about a person, but I can't say whether or not it's good. It is merciful to adopt an older dog because they are less likely to be adopted than a cute puppy, but it is probably evidence of impatience. It takes a lot of patience to train a puppy, especially potty training. When I was training a puppy named Mr. Ruffles, he kept peeing on my wood floors, and they had to get replaced. Some wood can fare better with acidity, but I had pine. Mahogany is stronger and would have fared better."

How he had not passed out yet was beyond me.

"Speaking of arboreal matters, I went to Redwood National Park recently, and the size of the Redwoods was incredible. Worth seeing if you haven't yet. Sadly, I was allergic to Redwood bark, and I was itching up a storm. My inflamed skin was red like that lamp over there." He pointed.

Every suspicious rash he'd ever had was now mine to imagine. He informed me that chewing gum was overrated, that goldsmiths should make a comeback, and that government propaganda deluded people into thinking that showering was necessary.

"I shower once a month and I'm as healthy as a horse. No one has complained about my musk. And I mean, look at you. You clearly don't *need* cosmetics, but that lipstick looks lovely on you. Eh, I mean . . ." He trailed off.

His silence startled me. It was the first lapse in conversation since he got over his rank finger pits. As the ringing in my ears subsided, I noticed his color-filled cheeks. Then, it dawned on me. What shorted him on words was not his lack of knowledge; it was complimenting a girl. The compliment had slipped through in the midst of his weird honesty, and now he was in uncharted territory. It made sense. Why else would he be signing up for Seminars?

His bashfulness struck me as strangely beautiful, but I was overwhelmed by my desire to save him from it.

"My dad thinks the moon landing was a hoax," I blurted.

He looked up with the bright eyes of a child. "Really? Only recently have I come to believe it myself. I mean, in 1969 there was a lot of pressure on the US to appear to be on top, but in reality . . ."

He spent the last half hour of our time together discussing the moon landing and all the different theories surrounding its supposed execution. At the end of the night, he smiled widely, shook my hand with his bleu-cheese fingers, and said with a definitive air, "When you are released, look me up and we can really get into the fast food industry during the Cold War."

CHAPTER 11

Donny

My next date was incredible.

A house salad with cucumbers so green it could make a girl blush! And beautiful homemade gnocchi drizzled with the happy tears of a thousand angels! Oh! And the garlic bread! If I had known such a thing existed, I would have lived differently, I tell you! I would have (*collapses into tears*) lived (*releases a long, guttural wail*) differently (*lies prostrate, weakly calling up to heaven*).

Then there was Donny.

His deep Boston accent was endearing at first, but after a while it became wicked hahd to decipha. Lucky for me, the climax of this illustrious date was not lost in translation. When I returned from the bathroom, he leaned toward me with a secret. His soggy, smoky breath, heavy against my ear, sent goose bumps up my neck.

"Ya look wicked awkwahd when you walk, but I think it's 'cause your propohtions are so good. Ya like a freakin' top heavy Barbie doll."

Like something out of a Jane Austen novel.

If she was plastered on Sam Adams.[5]

---

5 For what it's worth, I'd be more likely to read her drunken work.

CHAPTER 12

Cave Men and Unrequited Love

I lounged with Greg and the Decafers in my favorite place at Coffee: the serenity pond in the back of the courtyard. The entire courtyard was blacktop except for this small grassy knoll with a little maple tree and picture-perfect pond. We dipped our fingers in, the koi swimming gracefully under the man-made ripples. Their orange gills glowed neon against the dark rocks lining the bottom of the pond. There was something about being near living things that brought me peace. The rest of the courtyard was more often than not littered with dead chipmunks and birds, but the water seemed to protect the fish from the chemical plant's poisons.

The guards and non-Decafers were on the other side of the courtyard, out of earshot, making our little pond the perfect place to share our Seminar horror stories.[6]

"Then there was Adam." I showed them the missing four-inch chunk of my hair in the back of my head. "He pulled little

---

6 The Decafers knew that we couldn't discuss the Seminars with them, so they kept their distance. From past experience, we'd all learned there was nothing more annoying than approaching a group of Decafers and having them go silent until you finally left. Best to stay away.

scissors out of his pocket and filched it on his way back from the bathroom. For a shrine, I presume."

"That's not the only thing he's erecting in your honor," Nympho Yvette whooped. "HEY-OH!"

Greg's face was frozen in amusement. "Shit, Flo, how have you not fallen in love yet?"

A hot summer breeze blew; the pollen from the blooming ragweed ran its histamine fingers through my hair. "My criminality has left my heart hard and my libido flaccid."

"It's okay, Flo. One day your libido will be hard and your heart flaccid."

"Well, I'm excited to report that I educated my date on women's empowerment last night," Feminist Lorraine said proudly. "Can you believe he didn't know there's such a thing as spousal rape? He actually thought his wife didn't have a right to refuse sex."

"Wives can't say no, they're married," Greg said. "Isn't that the whole point?"

Susie the Strangler, Lovely Elizabeth, and I shook our heads in unison. *Stop while you're ahead, oh backward one.*

Feminist Lorraine swooped down like a hawk. "Women can say no to sex anytime they want, Greg, regardless of a marriage license. What if you loved your partner with all your heart? But let's say you were tired and sick, or just wanted to be left alone. How would you feel if she forced you to have sex?"

"Can't rape the willing."

Feminist Lorraine stood up. "I can't . . . not today . . ."

After she walked away, Greg turned back to me. "Just a heads up, I decided the first place I'm taking you when you get out is my home bar, Coaches."

"You need to apologize to her."

"To who?"

I shot him a withering look.

"To Lorraine?" he scoffed. "It's Lorraine."

"Still, you were being a turd biscuit," I said. Granted, "ignorant misogynist" might have been a more appropriate term, but "turd biscuit" would be easier for Greg to wrap his head around.

"No I wasn't! I was just—" He stopped, perhaps knowing after all these years that he wasn't going to sway me. "Fine, I'll say sorry, but first can I tell you about Coaches?"

"Yes, but apologize after."

"Okay, whatever. So Coaches has got twenty-five beers on tap, and a house whiskey that can make you go blind."

"How's their food?" I asked.

"Oh yeah, you don't drink," he recalled. "Lame."

Greg *knew* I didn't drink. I told him every time he raved about a seasonal beer or new liqueur, but I think he pretended to forget, hoping that the peer pressure would change my mind. The end game, I could only assume, was to get me hammered and film me drunkenly singing "Don't Stop Believin'" to a coat rack. Too bad it wasn't going to happen; I had a killer falsetto.

"Their wings are pretty good. Not good enough to blind you, but still good. Either way, I'm paying."

"Greg, that's unnecessary. I have money saved up; I can swing ten bucks for wings."

"First of all, I'll never make you pay when we go out. I'm a gentleman. Second, you've got to save your money for our other adventures."

I smiled uneasily. "All right."

"What about us, Mr. Gentleman?" Susie the Strangler said. "You don't want to hang out with us, too?"

"Y'all are going to murder your dates. So I'll be seeing you here."

"I don't know. Most of my dates have been very polite, well-dressed guys." Nympho Yvette flipped through The *Watchtower.* "Total prudes, though. Not one hot guy in this magazine they rave about."

"Most of mine are closet cases," said Susie the Strangler, rubbing a disintegrating leaf between her hands. "As if going on fake dates with a felon is a better option than marrying a nice man and adopting multi-ethnic kids. My granddaddy would roll over in his grave if he heard me say that, but times have changed."

"Were any of your dates gay, Florence?" Greg asked.

"I don't know, I didn't check."

"They probably were." Greg draped his arm over my shoulders. "At least I'm not a homo."

"Sure." Greg's small-town-cultivated homophobia was a battle not worth fighting against. Trust me, I had tried and failed.

"I'm as straight as they come."

"You better get going," I said, ruffled.

"All right." He removed his arm. "I'll take the hint. Time to make those bowls shine." He pulled a toilet-brush baton out of his over-sized jumpsuit pocket, and walked off whistling a country tune.

"Well," Susie the Strangler mumbled. "That was uncomfortable."

"OH YEAH? I DIDN'T NOTICE."

I wasn't an idiot. Greg's feelings were becoming increasingly difficult to deny. Despite the fact that he was arranged-marriage material, I didn't want to be in an actual relationship with him. But it seemed Greg and I weren't on the same page. Or even in the same book.

He was beginning to speak in terms of "us," and when a man un-ironically talks about accompanying you to Pottery Barn, you're in trouble.

But I hadn't addressed the issue explicitly. It was up to him to bring it up. Unfortunately, bringing it up would take maturity— a fine attribute Greg had never heard of, let alone possessed. So we were stuck in limbo: him flirting fruitlessly and me pretending not to notice.

Pretending not to notice, or the "Feigned Ignorance Is Bliss Approach," has been honed to perfection by womankind for millennia.

In fact, early Neanderthal cave art suggests unrequited love was the second-largest problem faced by those societies.[7] Thankfully, women have evolved from crushing the undesirable man's head with a rock to simply avoiding the conversation altogether.

Yet, with refinement comes criticism. Most critics harbor distaste for the subtly of the approach, but I argue that it's better than being cocky and assuming someone has feelings for you. Maybe he was staring at you because your random long chin hair reminds him of his dear old grandmother's long chin hair. Maybe he bought you that expensive perfume because you have body-odor issues. And maybe he gave you that sexually charged side hug because you had a spider on your arm and he wanted to squish it without alarming you. There could be a thousand explanations for why he does what he does! Let us set aside our egos so the men can be the ones to explain themselves!

(Pleassssse don't make us initiate the conversation. Pleasssse!)

---

7 The first-largest problem being wildebeest trampling their children.

CHAPTER 13
Bad Happenings on a Hot Summer Day

We waited silently in the threshold of Coffee's chapel. One by one, Officers Ryder and Bennett unlocked our handcuffs and released us into the candlelit sanctuary. We slipped off our shoes before scattering throughout the holy space to our assigned mats.

"Welcome, everyone," our instructor Charmaine chimed, her soft voice like a babbling brook. She was always calm and at peace, her movements fluid like those of a synchronized swimmer. I wondered idly how much marijuana I would have to smoke to get to that level of tranquility.

She dragged the last of the pews underneath the stained glass windows, dusting her hands off on her hemp shirt. "As always, we will begin our practice today by assuming child's pose."[8]

Yup. Coffee offered yoga. If you think that sounds like privileged nonsense . . . you'd be right. But of all the bizarre

---

8 I would liken child's pose to the move you do when you are done with life and just faceplant onto your floor.

therapies Coffee offered, yoga was the most legitimate. Don't believe me? Feel free to shadow either Cathartic Acupuncture Therapy (a small Middle Eastern man sticks needles into our faces) or Feline Maintenance Therapy (people from the surrounding towns bring in their cats and we cut their nails for free).

"Now into *Adho Mukha Śvānāsana*, or downward-facing dog," Charmaine continued peacefully. "Shift your weight forward and keep those abs tight."

My scrawny arms trembled pathetically as sweat began accumulating between my stomach rolls. I could imagine what we looked like to the officers watching us—a field of orange butts growing out of the chapel floor.

Thankfully, Officer Carmel wasn't working today. Unlike most of the officers, who did crossword puzzles on their phones during yoga, he watched. You could practically feel his eyes boring into your chakra.[9] But his staring wasn't the worst part. If it was just that, I'd get over it. It was the barely audible moaning, the low-pitched groaning that emitted from his pervert mouth every time we changed positions, that made my skin crawl.

"Keep your elbows in, Jessie," Charmaine sang. "Ten more seconds. Ten, nine, eight . . ."

My armpits already smelled like a Russian circus. Stupid commissary deodorant.

"Six . . ."

---

9 Whatever a chakra is.

I hated this. Why did she always count so slowwww?

"Three, two, one." Charmaine exhaled happily. "How are you doing, Florence? Looks like you're in a little bit of pain."

"Nah," I said, collapsing onto my mat. "Piece of cake."

"Piece of kale," she corrected with a smile. "Now, everyone, sit down and touch your toes."

My fingertips grazed my toes effortlessly. I was a weakling, but I was a flexible weakling.

Charmaine stood up quietly. "Now *slowly* lie all the way down, feeling each muscle relax as you do. Today, we are going to do something a little different." She lifted a small vial out of her canvas bag. "We are going to do aromatherapy with the help of essential oils. If you aren't familiar with essential oils, they can do a whole host of things, like foster relaxation and increase blood flow." She unscrewed the vial's cap. "I will be coming around and putting a drop on each of your foreheads. It's mixed with carrier oil, so it is safe to apply to your skin."

She tiptoed around in her hippy elf-shoes, touching each prisoner's forehead with the smelly concoction. I dreaded the migraine this bohemia potion was going to give me.

She leaned over me and dabbed it between my eyes. I was relieved. The smell wasn't overpowering, and in fact, it was rather pleasant.

All of a sudden, my throat tightened spastically. My eyes sprang open as I struggled for breath. My lungs yearned for oxygen, but I could only get wisps of air.

HOLY SHIT. I WAS ALLERGIC TO THIS DEVIL ELIXIR.

In a panic, I racked my brain for anything I could remember about allergic reactions. The only thing that came to mind was the movie *My Girl*, and SHE DIED.

I needed an EpiPen and fast. If I didn't get one, they'd find my lifeless body and assume that I'd reached a yogic Nirvana so great that I simply crossed over to the Great Beyond.

How was this happening? I wasn't allergic to anything. Not that I knew of, anyways.

Then a light bulb flickered on. The swelling in my throat wasn't swelling at all; it was an unbearable lump of sorrow.

Something about this satanic essential oil was sending me into a deep, bottomless depression. But why? What was the scent?

It was familiar, but I couldn't place it. It wasn't cinnamon or chamomile. Not lemongrass or mint. What was it? What was th—?

Lavender.

I immediately plugged my nose and began mouth breathing.

"Lose yourself in the smell," Charmaine said dreamily. "Let it transport you to the fields of lavender in France. The sun is shining warm on your face. You are safe. You have nowhere to go, nowhere to be. You are just here in this field, enjoying the beauty."

But I was not in France. Charmaine's desolation oil had taken me back six years, to a day I'd give my right ovary to forget.

The sun's cancerous light woke me that morning. I looked over to his empty side of bed. As always, he had already left for work, and as always, I was running late. I tied my hair into a messy bun, threw on my daycare polo, and raced to my car.

My day was filled with the usual children's giggles, sticky fingers, and loaded diapers. After noses were wiped, spitty Cheerios cleaned up, and the children homeward bound, I swan-dived onto my couch, exhausted. I napped until the intermittent gusts of the fan weren't enough to fight the August heat.

"Hi sleepyhead!" My best friend Holly knocked at my screen door, bearing a bouquet of flowers. "Special delivery!"

Drowsily, I swung my sweaty legs over the cushion's edge. "Come on in."

"Good to see you, my dear." Her miniature flaxen ponytail bounced as she walked in. She was tiny, cute, and energetic—like a human Pomeranian.

She handed me the flowers, and I gave her with a hug.

"Ew. No offense, but you are really sweaty."

"Sorry." I yawned, sniffing my armpit. "I should probably reapply."

"Keep these nearby, and no one will notice your raunchy odor." Holly laughed, handing me the bouquet. "A couple left it at the shop. It's a sample for their wedding next year. It's a little foo-foo, but whatever."

I breathed in the bouquet. Lavender. I cherished the sweet smell for a moment. "Thank you. They're beautiful."

Holly had spent the last year working at a high-end flower shop, and she was always bringing me pricey bouquets that rich people accidentally left behind. Fun fact: when it comes to flowers, rich people have great taste and bad memories.

I filled up a cheap plastic vase and set the elegant lavender bouquet inside. I could almost hear it objecting to being showcased in such a lowbrow vessel.

"It's smoldering in here," Holly complained. "If I don't get something to drink in the next ten seconds, I'm going to die."

"Sorry," I said, filling a glass of water. "Maybe next summer we'll get an air conditioner. I don't know though, it's so bad for the environment."

"You guys are still on that environmental kick?" She chugged the water, wiping the rogue droplets off her chin.

"You could say that. Him more than me."

"Well, it's supposed to be even hotter tomorrow, so if you guys want come over for dinner, we'll be blasting the AC. We have zero respect for the environment."

"I'm in." I leaned over to smell the beautiful lavender bouquet again. "If you need help cooking, let me know."

"Why don't we let the boyfriends barbeque while we drink sangria and get white-girl drunk?"

"YES."

"Speaking of boyfriends, where's yours? He's usually home by now."

In retrospect, there were small moments leading up to it: hearing about his promotion through a mutual friend, glimpsing a number I didn't recognize on his phone, eating a few more dinners alone because he was "working overtime." Each an intrinsically harmless happenstance easily attributed to forgetfulness or bad gas. But, at that moment, I learned the truth. Because, at that moment, I found The Letter taped to the fridge.

He was honest and straightforward on that flimsy notebook paper. It was not another woman. It was The Other Woman. The One he loved before and Who loved him once more, and for three years I had been falling asleep to a heart that beat for Her.

The smell of lavender seared my nose, my throat, my gut, my chest.

"Florence?"

My eyes flitted open. A blurry outline of Charmaine stood over me.

"Are you okay?"

"I'm fine," I lied, wiping the tears from my face. "I'm—I'm allergic to lavender. It makes my eyes water."

"Oh no! You should've said something!" She grabbed her sweat towel and wiped off my forehead. "Officer Ryder, take her to the infirmary."

Officer Ryder walked me down the hall, periodically assessing me out of the corner of his eye, no doubt making sure

I didn't go into anaphylactic shock on his watch. I ignored him, plodding on. When we reached the infirmary, he waved to Nurse Shelly, who was texting with her feet up on her desk, not paying attention. He shrugged and left. Normally, guards are mandated to stay in a room with a civilian, but Nurse Shelly was no civilian. She was an ex-cop and a hardy woman at that. She could put a broad down.

As I lowered myself onto one of the beds, I wondered if she was a better cop than a nurse. She hadn't looked up since I had come in, still absorbed in whatever text battle she was in. Judging by the way she scrunched up her mouth and pounded her meaty thumbs into her phone, the argument wasn't going well.

I refocused on the drop ceiling of the infirmary and tried counting its pockmarks. Somehow, the hospital bed was less comfortable then my own cell bed. How was that possible? What was the thread count of these sheets? Ten?

Didn't matter. This was a low point.

My past was infiltrating my life—in broad daylight. Nighttime was fair game, but now it was ambushing me while the sun was up. He left me for Her—it's the same reality I'd been living with for years. Why couldn't my subconscious let it go?! But no, my subconscious needed to bring it out dramatically... with witnesses and all! It was embarrassing. As the years passed, things were supposed to get easier. The past was supposed to fade into oblivion, but no, She was as front-and-center as ever.

What was wrong with me? Why couldn't I get over it?

I bet She was resilient after breakups, and I'd go double or nothing that She'd never had a public meltdown during yoga. Hell, She probably taught yoga and could do *Pungu Mayurasana* with Her eyes closed! She was amazing, and I was just a basket case who was obsessing about my dead boyfriend's new girlfriend—a certifiable train wreck.

Tears trickled down my cheeks. *Suck it up, Florence, keep it together.*

"Hey," Nurse Shelly yelled, "you're going to need a couple Benadryl if your eyes are still watering that much."

I didn't even fight her. I took the pills and drifted off.

CHAPTER 14

Vincent

The next morning, Officer Ramsey beat his baton against the bars of my cell. "Rise and shine, bitch."

"LET ME DIEEEE," I groaned drowsily.

I was kidding, of course, because I was pretty sure I was already dead.

The nurse had given me three Benadryl capsules for my fake lavender allergy, and I was having the worst antihistamine hangover of my life. My muscles were sore, my spit tasted toxic, and my armpit smell had evolved into what I would deem "Turkish Bathhouse."

My condition only deteriorated as lavender continued to haunt me with The Letter on its coattails. It's a sad irony that I had never succeeded in memorizing a single quote from Shakespeare, but I had managed to permanently etch The Letter into my mind. Even as I tried to distract myself, the most painful lines ate away at me.

Believe me when I say I don't wish to cause you pain. She is the loveliest, most wonderful creature I've ever encountered, and only for her would I risk hurting you. I hope that brings you some comfort.

Comfort indeed! I was worried that I had competed with her and lost, but now I understood: there was no competition at all. She was cosmic goodness incarnate, and I was a dungeon troll.

But why dwell on it? The past was dead and so was he.

Needless to say, after hours of this mental torture, I was grateful when Officer Ramirez retrieved me for my Decaf Seminar. I was desperate to get out of my head and into someone else's world—whatever that was.

If my date liked golf, I'd rant with him about the increasingly poor maintenance of courses. If he loved *Star Wars,* I'd delve into the nuances of Alderaan's trade law. If he had a milk allergy, I'd spend the whole night comparing and contrasting almond, rice, coconut, and soy milk. I was in it to win it.

"Hi, I'm Vincent."

I flashed my most winning smile. "I'm Florence. How are you doing?"

"Wonderful, thank you."

Vincent was sporting a chiseled jawline, designer scruff, and perfectly coiffed hair. He wasn't just easy on the eyes; he was downright tingly in the loins. Seriously. This joker looked like a young Liam Neeson . . . which begged The Question. The Question Above All Questions: What was wrong with him that he was spending a Friday night in a Rehabilitation Seminar?

The Question no sooner crossed my mind than I felt someone hovering over our table. I glanced up to see a slim, beautiful woman with a long fishtail braid standing confidently before us. Her shoulders were drawn back, a baby carrier dangling on her left arm.

"Hello?"

She ignored me. "Vincent."

His movie star eyes rose slowly to meet her gaze. "Mary, what are you doing here?"

"He's your son too," she answered poignantly.

AW SHIZ! WE GOT SOME JERRY SPRINGER UP IN HURRR!!

"Mary," Vincent warned.

She scanned me over. "Does she know?"

He didn't answer.

"That's a no." She swung the baby carrier onto the table. It landed with an audible thud. "This is Theodore, Vincent's son."

Inside the carrier lay a baby fresh out of the womb, sleeping with his tiny fists tucked under his chin. His golden brown hair, the same as Vincent's, lay perfectly against his little head. His lips pouted slightly as he dreamt his infant dreams. He was the type of irresistible Gerber baby that tricks you into having kids of your own.

"Hi, Theo," I obliged. "Sorry we had to meet under these circumstances."

Vincent ran his fingers through his hair. "Can we not do this, Mar?"

"Don't call me that. Are you really so self-absorbed that you can't make time for him?"

"This isn't about him."

Her eyes welled up with tears. "He is the only thing it's about anymore! That's what you don't get!"

All of a sudden, Mary bent over, her lips against my ear. "It's easy to fall in love with him, but he'll never be able to love anyone more than himself."

Before I could reply, Officer Ramirez approached her. "Ma'am, you can't be here."

Mary straightened up, lifting Theo's carrier off the table. "I was leaving." As she headed to the door, I could hear her talking to the carrier. "I'm tired too, bubby. Let's go home."

Officer Ramirez scratched his head. "Everything all right here?"

"Just my ex-wife, officer."

The officer shrugged dully and walked away. In his wake, the waitress took our orders.

When we were finally alone, I cocked my head. "Your ex-wife, eh?"

"Yeah." He paused. "Well, technically my current wife. I haven't filed the papers yet, but as you can probably tell, it's not going to come as a surprise."

"What happened there?"

"You don't want to talk about my problems. Let's talk about you. Tell me about yourself and how you've developed into the person you are."

"Nope. We're going to talk about your baby momma comin' up here makin' accusations." *Because I've finally found something to distract me from lavender.*

"It's a long story. I want to hear about your strengths and your—"

"Nope. Don't care."

"Fine," he said reluctantly. "I guess it would help to explain that I have my own private counseling practice. I counsel people with ODD, OCD, and RAD. Anyways, Mary came in as a client about a year ago—"

"You had sex with a client?" I asked, incredulous.

"Not exactly," he said hesitantly.

"Well . . ." I laughed. "Unless she is a ninja with a turkey baster, you had sex with her."

He shifted uncomfortably.

"Oh."

"What?"

"Did she . . . rape you?" I asked seriously.

"Not technically. I mean, she seduced me after I had gotten out of a bad relationship." He shook his head. "I was in a vulnerable place, and I shouldn't have been making sexual decisions at the time."

"Oh." I sighed in relief. "Well, we all make stupid decisions when we're vulnerable. You can't blame her for that."

If I had a dollar for every sexual misadventure I had after my breakup . . . I'd be on welfare. Not a lot of guys were buying what I was selling, BUT a valet accidentally brushed my boob once, and I'm counting it.

"That's true. I will take equal responsibility for our tryst." He rubbed his hands on his perfectly fitted jeans. "When she told me she was pregnant, I did the right thing and married her so she wasn't marginalized as an unwed mother. But she was incredibly ungrateful."

"Would you rather she kiss your ring?"

"No," he said, "but I'm tired of her pressuring me to be the perfect father. She jumps down my throat because I'm not always home to take care of the kid."

"You guys are still living together?"

"For now." He began biting his pinky nail. "You have to understand, I'm an introvert. I can't be emotionally present one hundred percent of the time."

"I don't know what that means."

"It means I have limited emotional resources. I have to budget my time wisely so I don't get burnt out."

"How much time do you 'budget' to Theo?" I asked.

"I've never quantified it." He furrowed his brow. "If I were forced to put a number to it, I'd say about an hour or two every other afternoon." He paused. "No . . . well . . . yeah. Give or take."

"You three live in the same house, and you see him one hour every other afternoon?"

"Give or take."

"What the hell do you do when you're avoiding your wife and your kid at home?"

"I'm not 'avoiding them,'" he shot back defensively. "When I'm home, I am in what I call 'recharge mode.' I counsel the needy and broken all day, so when I get home it's imperative that I spend time caring for myself."

"Chronically masturbating?"

"No! Listening to music, writing, and things like that. If I took care of the kid all the time, my emotional energy would be constantly depleted. Mary doesn't understand that." He sighed. "Then again, she is just that kind of woman."

"What kind is that?"

"Troubled. She is unsympathetic. She has issues. Many issues. I should have known how truly troubled she was."

I massaged my forehead. He was giving me a headache. "I hate to break it to you, but you're the one with the serious issues."

"What?" Vincent was clearly offended. "How?"

"Sweet baby angel." I grimaced. "You had sex with a client, and you married her because she was pregnant. Now, you're getting divorced because you're a deadbeat dad. EXAMINE YOUR LIFE."

"You're hurting my feelings."

"I'm not trying to be cruel, but you are selfish."

"Why? Because I won't wake up in the middle of the night and change the kid's diaper? That makes me selfish?"

"First off, his name is Theo. AND YES. You live in the same house! Do you really not help with him in the middle of the night?"

"If I sacrifice my sleep, I may not be able to properly counsel my clients. That could result in lives being lost."

"You have the biggest God-complex I have ever seen."

"Nuh-uh." I had heard that tone many times over the years, usually from three-year-olds denying they stole their friend's toy.

"Come on. Why do you think you are sitting here today? You came here to save me from my corrupted criminal spirit."

"Is that such a bad thing?" He whipped out those puppy-dog eyes, but they had no power over me.

"Yeah," I said curtly, "when you're doing it to distract yourself from the fiery wreck that is your life."

"I—"

"Trying to help other people when you can't maintain a relationship with your wife or your son doesn't make you a hero."

"I work with people who struggle with terrible mental health afflictions."

"You're one bad fortune cookie away from a complete mental breakdown yourself."

"No—"

"You can't handle a relationship outside of work, either because intimacy scares you or you're too selfish to care for someone on a day-to-day basis. Either way, that's a personality disorder waiting to be diagnosed."

Vincent didn't respond.

"The truth is that you are going to end up alone in this world with nothing more than a fleeting feeling that you fucked up. And you'll be right."

I waited for him to defend himself with more of his sad rationalizations, but he didn't.

Instead, he cried.

CHAPTER 15

A Half-Assed Explanation

The next day, I awoke with an unbearable feeling in the pit of my stomach. No doubt Dr. Sean had heard about last night's catastrophe. He was probably already planning an intervention, with my family tearfully reading the letters they wrote about how my reckless behavior was destroying them. All the while I'd be sitting in the corner, biting my fingernails, trying to explain myself. Because, believe it or not, there was an explanation for my seemingly bitchy behavior.

After he left me for Her, I got an ill-fated perm, bought heels I never wore, and tried to "get myself out there," which consisted of going on dates with a variety of guys like Vincent.

At first, it was refreshing to talk to men who were so attentive and so empathetic. But eventually, they'd convince me that my sixth-grade teacher's derogatory comment about my puppy drawing still hurt and that they were the only one in the world capable of understanding that. (Because no one better understands pain than upper-class suburban white men with college degrees and intact families.) Then they would say that I was sapping their emotional energy and that they needed time to work on themselves. After my third encounter with a Vincent-type, I lost all patience for dealing with these emotionally intense asshats.

Of course, that explanation wouldn't go over well in an intervention. Especially since everything in my past was supposed to be so far dead and buried that it was like it never happened at all. I could imagine Dr. Sean using the word "transference" with a furrowed brow.

I needed a plan. I couldn't go down without a fight.

Maybe if I blamed it on my Tourette's syndrome, they'd cut me some slack. Oh, have I not mentioned that I have Tourette's syndrome? Silly me. I probably I forgot to tell you because I absolutely do not have it. But Dr. Sean didn't know that . . . unless he took four seconds to look at my medical records. Shit. Damn it. Son of a bitch. Penis face. Why the hell couldn't I have fucking Tourette's?

All I had was a family history of flat feet and strokes.

. . . wait . . .

That was it!

Strokes! Strokes are serious shit. Granted, I wasn't slurring my words and had no hemiparesis . . . but . . . um, a stroke can manifest itself as a severe headache. Yeah. And Dr. Sean couldn't have known that I had a splitting headache yesterday because I braved it without complaint. But I mean if I had to describe it, I'd have to say it was a pretty "stroke-y" headache; so stroke-y that it triggered my undiagnosed, latent Tourette's syndrome. So, yeah, I'm pretty much a hero for having survived such a horrific ordeal. Poor Vincent was merely a casualty of a wildly unfortunate medical emergency.

Yeah, that would work. Or it wouldn't, and I'd end up in a state penitentiary for three to five decades.

Just the thought of that sent me darting to the toilet. Stress™, allowing you to keep that beach body since the fall of man.[10]

My b-hole and I spent the morning oscillating between panicked anxiety and survivalist rationalization until the Warden unlocked my cell with a sadistic smile plastered on his face.

"Dr. Sean needs to see you." His lips glistened with spit. Fat bastard was literally licking his chops at the thought of me getting in trouble.

I took a deep breath. *Let's party.*

---

10 If there was one thing I learned about the human condition while at Coffee, it was that pooping is the true Great Equalizer. Whether you poop in a gold-lined porcelain commode or a plastic grocery bag on State Street, you're still pooping. The most uncomfortable week of my life was spent, cheeks clenched, avoiding the sorrel toilet in the corner of my cell. When the only accessible toilet is within earshot of everyone in a fifteen-foot radius, the dread of near-public pooping will keep your sphincter nice and tight. In case you're worried, I eventually gave in to nature and have been pooping ever since. Thanks for your concern!

CHAPTER 16

Intervention

The Warden shoved me into Dr. Sean's office. "I believe this belongs to you."

I stood like a prized cow in front of the giant mahogany desk. The Warden snapped his fingers and pointed to the chair. "Sit down."

"Thank you," Dr. Sean said tersely. "I've got it from here. Please close the door on your way out."

The Warden reluctantly ducked out, unhappy to miss my flogging.

"You've been here for almost five years." Dr. Sean leaned back in his chair and stretched. "It's been a long haul." I looked around for teary-eyed family members ready to intervene, but it was just the good doctor and I.

With less eyes and expectations upon him, his professional disposition abated. His unclenched jaw revealed him to be a man no older than me, with potential for a sink filled with dirty dishes waiting for him at home. "Are you ready to be out of here?"

I hated when shrinks did this. Come out and say it. Don't make me *own* it. "You and I both know that I'm not getting out of here."

"Why not?"

"Please don't play dumb," I begged.

"Okay, let's talk about last night. I want to hear your side of the story before I read the evaluation."

I eyed him skeptically. "If you didn't read the evaluation, how'd you know to call me in here?"

"I overheard the officers say that one of the prisoners made a Seminar volunteer cry."

"And what? It had to be me?"

He looked at me as if to say, *DUHHHH, you impulsive idiot.*

"Okay, fine."

"What did you do to make"—Dr. Sean opened the file in front of him and checked the name—"Vincent cry?"

"I showed him a collection of poems I wrote."

"Florence—"

"He told me it was the most soulful poetry he'd ever read. I told him it was in the beginning stages, but he insisted that I share it with the world. He said the fate of the human race depended on it. I feel like he was exaggerating, but people can interpret my work as they wish."

Dr. Sean sighed. "We've talked about this before; sarcasm hinders communication. Stop using it, and tell me what happened."

I walked toward the barred window, watching the parking lot below. It was comforting to think that I was only three stories and one cinderblock wall away from hopping in a car and driving away.[11] "He was an emotional basket case."

"Did you threaten him or physically assault him?"

"Don't you think you would've heard if I physically assaulted someone?"

"Maybe, but until you tell me what went on, I can't help you." He took off his thin-framed glasses and rubbed his eyes. "I know you don't see merit in our sessions, but if you want to complete the program, you need to cooperate with me."

"Fine," I conceded. "He was a self-pitying guy with a messiah complex, so I called him out on it, which, in retrospect, may have offended his male sensibility."

"You know, it's best not to offend male sensibility during these things." A look of uncertainty shadowed his face. "Florence, the purpose of Decaffeination is to make sure you aren't regressing."

Fear crept up my throat. "So I'm not getting out of here?"

"It's one evaluation," he assured me.

"Come on, you and I both know that one bad evaluation is enough to get kicked out."

"You are allowed to have off days, Florence."

"Am I though? You said it yourself. That's evidence of regression."

"I'm not worried. If you were to make this a habit, then we'd have to talk."

---

11 An in-depth knowledge of hot-wiring would probably be helpful too.

"How do I know you aren't lying in order to keep me de-escalated?"

Dr. Sean laughed. "You've been in therapy too long."

"That's not an answer."

"You are *not* getting kicked out of Decaffeination because of this. Do you want it in writing?"

"If you're offering."

Dr. Sean rolled his eyes, something he usually reserved for Nympho Yvette's over-the-top sexual comments. "If it was up to me, you would have been released years ago, so I don't intend to expel you from the Decaf program."

He was lying. If he wanted me released years ago, I would've been. The Rehabilitation Board bases its decisions off Dr. Sean's recommendations. "Whatever you say."

"Just don't do it again, okay? Lie low, and you'll get through this."

"Okay," I replied, completely unconvinced.

He closed the folder dramatically. "All right then, enough of that! Now, have the Rehabilitation Seminars changed your feelings about dating? As of our last session, you were feeling sour toward the idea of romantic relationships."

"Ha. My feelings remain quite the same. It was a fun season of my life, but now onto cat collecting and Netflix."

"Don't give up on relationships. You've learned a lot about yourself in your time here. In the future, you'll know who you are and what's good for you . . ."

"Sure."

Laura Weber

"We aren't bringing in the cream of the crop here. The goal of Decaffeination is to expose you to different personalities."

"Yep. I know."

"I know your relationship with—"

"Is it okay if we don't talk about him today?"

Dr. Sean nodded, looking up at the ceiling. "Okay, let's take another approach. Tell me what, in a future paramour, would allow you to be vulnerable again?"

"Is it all right if I go back to my cell?" I asked.

I was never keen on talking to Dr. Sean about *opening myself to love*. I had seen the pictures of him and his wife. They were clearly high school sweethearts who had gotten married the summer after college and had their first kid a year after that. He didn't know the first thing about having his heart pulverized, let alone risking that again.

"Yes, that's fine. I'll get Officer Lenny to take you back."

Later that evening, I heard a light rapping on my cell door. I walked over to see a figure sprawled on the floor. "Help," it whimpered. "I've fallen and I can't get up."

I nudged the figure with the tip of my foot. "I think you're going to live, sir."

Greg pushed himself up. "Word on the block is that you saw Dr. Sean today."

"Yeah." I sat down, back to back with Greg, divided by the cold metal bars. "I got in trouble for upsetting one of the Seminar guys."

"What did you do?"

78

"I don't want to rehash it. Let's just say that it's not enough to get me kicked out of Decaf, according to Dr. Sean."

"Reassuring," Greg said sarcastically. "Florence, you need to watch yourself in these stupid Seminars."

"Don't need another lecture. I get that my actions were 'unacceptable.'"

"You mean you *aren't* supposed to make grown men cry?"

I groaned. "You heard about it?"

"You're the talk of the town, my love." Greg turned around and leaned in. "Seriously though, be careful. They will send you to a state prison to cover their asses. They don't want word getting out that one of their 'rehabilitated' prisoners is still a . . . what's the clinical term? Mean old bat?"

"Ha, ha."

"It would be a PR nightmare."

"I couldn't see the Warden letting that happen," I agreed reluctantly.

"Um, yeah. Remember three and a half years ago, when he took away your phone privileges for two weeks just because you hung up too loud?"

"How do you remember that kind of stuff? I can barely remember what I had for breakfast."

"You had oatmeal—like you do every day. And listen to me: the Warden's got a short fuse. Don't give him a reason to kick you out."

"Okay, I get it. I promise, I will be an upstanding, respectable prisoner from here on out."

"Better be, because if you get shipped off to a real state prison, it'd be a real pain in the butt."

"Yeah, yeah."

"I'm not joking. I'm locked into a year-long lease, and I'll lose my deposit if I have to follow you to another prison in BF Maine."

"I get it." I walked to my bed and lay down. "I'm going to bed."

"It's only eight o'clock."

"Still, I'm tired."

"Come on," he whined.

He wasn't one for subtly.

I put my pillow over my head. "Good night, Greg."

CHAPTER 17

Kev

The following week, I awaited my suitor with a new resolution for peacekeeping. I was not going to get kicked out of Decaf because I couldn't play nice. How hard could it be not to verbally accost my Decaf date for two hours?

As if the universe accepted my challenge, the bell above the door tolled loudly. A lean, greasy man sporting a sparse black mustache and a Mickey Mouse sweatshirt entered. He fist-bumped the officers as he handed them a pink sheet of paper. They pointed to me, and he waltzed over with the swagger of a rodeo clown.

"Evenin', darlin'. How goes it?"

"It's going well," I replied, shaking his calloused hand. "And you are?"

"Kev."

"Nice to meet you, Kevin."

"It's Kev, sweetheart," he said.

"Oh—sorry, Kev."

He plopped down in his chair. "Don't wear it out. You know what you're feastin' on tonight?"

"I'm getting the filet mignon."

"Fay-lay min-yawn? Aren't we hoity-toity?" Kev tucked his napkin into his sweatshirt collar. "I'm not into all that materialist crap."

Unsure of how to respond to such a ridiculous comment, I powered through. "What are you in the mood for, then?"

"I'm just getting the B-B-Q ham-pepperoni-sausage sammich."

"So you're a vegetarian," I tried joking.

"Hell no! From the rooter to the tooter, I'll eat the whole pig."

"Ha, I get that."

But I didn't. Kev's words were coated in indecipherable hillbilly slang that only got worse throughout the night.

"So I just got done running my boys all over town," he said at one point.

I stared at him blankly. Was this some farmhand term for streaking?

"I'm a track coach, hon."

"Oh," I said, pleasantly surprised. "How do you motivate them? What's your strategy?"

"I dunno? I tell them to run, and they run." He flicked something out of his nose with his pinky. "It ain't rocket science."

That I believed.

"All our teams are gunna take the championships this year," he said, throwing an invisible football across the room. "Ya know, I was a running back in my heyday."

"No kidding."

He leaned back, checking out my cankles under the table. "I'm assumin' you weren't a cheerleader."

"Nope," I said, biting my tongue. *Down, girl. You need to stay friendly.*

I took a deep breath. "No, not a cheerleader. I did theater at my high school." *How's that for a graceful recovery?* "We had a good theater program. My parents and cousins came to all my shows."

"Cousins?" He winked as the waitress arrived with our meals. "Gotcha."

"Yeah."

"Say no more." He raised his eyebrows suggestively. "We all got 'em."

"I guess . . . if your parents' siblings have kids . . ."

"Listen, sweetheart. It's only incest if you go all the way."

My jaw fell open.

"What?" he snorted. "You got somethin' to say?"

All of a sudden, a hot, nervous feeling crept up my cheeks. I had to stay on his good side even if it killed me.

"Oh, ah," I stammered, "sorry, it's just that—I thought it was only incest if you got pregnant."

"I wish! I woulda only been charged twice. Enough about family." He lifted his sweatshirt to wipe barbecue sauce off his face, exposing a thick un-happy trail to hell. "Now, I gotta know, how many chick fights do you see a week?"

"Um, Tuesday is burrito day, and the lines can get pretty heated?"

"Ah, 'burrito day.' Your man pieces visit, eh? I bet you go buck wild. The quiet ones always do. Little hair pullin'? Scratchin'? I can see you got a lot pent up. I mean, I saw the way you were looking at me when I came in." He motioned to his emaciated body. "Can't blame you."

I was sure he was quite a catch at the meth labs he frequented.

"Tell me every dirty detail of what you want to do to me. Spare no nitty-gritty."

Before answering, I took a moment to center. As Charmaine said in yoga, you have to find your breath, and focus on its flow.

In, out.

In, out.

My annoyance was ebbing away, and my heart was filling with patience, good will, and—Kev caressed my hand.

Nope.

"I wouldn't touch you with a ten-foot pole, you PBR-chugging hillbilly," I growled.

He shot back in his chair. "Oh Mamacita, I knew you were holding back!" He chuckled. "But I ain't no PBR drinker. I'm a Bud Light man from the womb to the tomb."

"Fetal alcohol syndrome might explain some things."

"You've got some thoughts about me, little lady." He rolled up his sweatshirt sleeves. "Let's hear 'em."

"You sure? The last time I told someone what I thought of him, he cried. Over there." I pointed. "At that table."

"Darlin', you couldn't make me cry if you rubbed an onion in my eye."

"You asked for it," I said, resigned. "First off, I assume you have webbed feet due to inbreeding."

"Not true since the surgery. What else you got?"

"My guess is that you live in a trailer with an ironing board that doubles as a kitchen table."

"Grilled cheese, baby: two birds, one stone."

"I bet your kids are in prison and you've had more than one birthday party at a strip club."

"My birthdays are the reason that most of my kids are in prison!" He laughed. "Hate to break it to you, darlin', but we ain't that different!"

"Yeah." I rolled my eyes. "Minus the hepatitis, I'm sure we are *very* similar."

"You know what, baby girl, it's my turn to guess. I think that someone dumped your sweet ass for another piece of sweet ass, and that's why you got a chip on your shoulder."

Huh. For being the inbred offspring of a NASCAR cult leader, he was surprisingly intuitive. But the way he drew out his *r*'s made me want to jam an ice pick into my ear, so I wasn't giving him that one.

"Wrong," I lied. "Tell me about the lovely honky-tonk bar-huggers you pick up. Are they fair game as long as they've got half their teeth and speak English?"

"Well, I ain't cartin' home no immigrant!"

"Just the illegal ones? Or do you hate everyone who didn't grow up within a mile of you? And, I hate to break it to you, *darlin'*, but unless your ancestors were Native American, you're technically an immigrant."

"HA!" He guffawed. "That kind of ignorant attitude is the reason women can't vote."

"Really, Gunther?"

"The name's Kev, princess."

"Sorry, Jethro."

After what felt like a thousand years, our Seminar came to an end.

"Good night, you stuck up twit," he howled.

"Sweet dreams, you backwater lowbrow bastard."

Some say that the line between love and hate is thin, like fishing wire barely visible from the dock.

But those people are stupid.

The distance between love and hate is expansive, but I knew I had landed favorably on Kev's spectrum. How? Because the blood-quickening electricity that made us want to smack each other would make for an impressive, and, no doubt, sexually-charged evaluation.

That, or he would say I was a volatile woman with an unchecked impulse-control problem. It wouldn't be the first time someone argued that point.

Twelve jurors bought it.

CHAPTER 18

Why I Stopped Drinking, and Why I Should Probably Start Again

After reading The Letter, I spent six weeks in my foster mother's care. She kissed my wounds and gently lulled me to sleep every night. Her alcohol content was 9.5%, and I dove into her amber body until I couldn't feel mine. In those moments between waking and slumber, not only did I understand the drunkard's haven, I retreated to its hoppy sanctuary frequently and with great relish.

But God, in his pine-scented office, orchestrated a plan to thwart my alcoholism. He blessed me with a stomach that, when alcohol was added, grew a merciless, spiteful gremlin. From the first sip to the hangover, I was deathly nauseous. And in those six weeks, I pled night and day that the belly-dwelling gremlin would leave me alone and let me drink in peace, but after offering my first-born child innumerable times, no bargain could be reached.[12] So I reluctantly heeded the divine message and wallowed in sober sadness.

Admittedly, sadness is a pretty vanilla term for what I was experiencing. Not only did the man I loved leave me for Another Woman, but I lost my home. The cute little home that we rented, the one we got permission from our landlord to paint, the one we filled with the aromas of our homemade meals. Our home was now *their* home. I couldn't bring myself to go back, so my best friend Holly volunteered to get my things. When she returned, she said my ex had already packed my stuff up, and she handed me two garbage bags filled with my things. Yep, my stuff was trash to him, and Her stuff was hanging in our closet. I dragged the bags into Holly's spare bedroom, face-planted on the bed, and sobbed.

Most nights, I would lie awake too tired to cry. I would listen to the porch steps creak under the weight of some unseen serial killer. I would think bitterly, *You want to do this, Murderer McAssassin? I've got nothing to lose. I WILL TAKE YOU.* But as quickly as my blood boiled, it would cool pathetically, and I'd resign myself to my fate, think, *Eh, it's fine, you can murder me, and fall asleep.*

My rage-despair pendulum swung dramatically in the following months. Holly was gracious and empathetic, but she was ready to get away. Therefore, when her demented grandmother

---

12 Billy, your mother and I need to talk to you. Years ago, your mother made an agreement with a belly-dwelling gremlin. Ha, you're going to laugh when you hear this. She, uh, yeah, well she promised him that he could have you. So we love you, but a deal's a deal. Bundle up. He's waiting outside. And don't look him in the eye. He hates that.

in the middle of nowhere Pennsylvania walked to a Bob Evans in nothing but Birkenstocks, she jumped at the chance to visit her family.

Unfortunately, it robbed me of Friday night plans and a corroborating witness.

The day Holly returned, we were met with the ugly news of my ex's murder. My reaction was succinct and robotic. I grabbed my jacket and a copy of *The Best of Sylvia Plath*, and I went off the grid for two days. I don't know where I went or what I did, but from the tokens I have from that time, it appears I made lanyards.

Lots of lanyards.

Things swiftly went downhill from there.

Despite Holly's initial support, when the shit hit the fan, she went from being the cute human Pomeranian I described earlier to a full-out punt-able Pomeranian asshole.

Apparently, she had known for a while that I was a mentally ill murderer, and things were finally "adding up." Holly sat our friends down and explained that my nightly bathroom visits, "obsession" with scented candles, and (wildly unfortunate) habit of finding dead mice in the basement were the trifecta of psychopathy. My friends were equal parts horrified and convinced.

Just goes to show that a semester of criminal psychology at the University of Phoenix makes you just stupid enough to be believable.

In the end, I really didn't care. If she needed my tragic life story to make herself seem interesting, she was pathetic enough as it was. SO, YOU'RE WELCOME, HOLLY, FOR MAKING YOU SEEM COOL. IT SHOULD HOLD YOU OVER UNTIL YOU GET A HOBBY. OR GOUT.

All that to say, I braved the legal system with no one but my distraught parents.

You know, it's about time you met the 'rents.

CHAPTER 19

Visiting Day: Don't Feed the Prisoners

In the cold hours of the morning, we gathered under warm waterfalls like a pack of furry albino grizzlies. It was a myriad of floppy boobs, unshaved muffs, and dimply butts. It's funny how people assume that prison showers are erotic and fun. I blame it on *Orange Is the New Black*; all that steamy cunnilingus got people muddled. The reality is that prison showers are seedy like a YWCA locker room, and the only moaning heard is from the horror of dropping bar soap on the disgusting hairy tile. Thing looked like a vitamin-deficient Furby when you picked it back up.

A half hour later, a river of freshly showered inmates fanned into the visitation room, each claiming a stainless steel table. The crisscross metal seat seared ice cold through my jumpsuit. I watched as a smorgasbord of parents, boyfriends, girlfriends, tennis partners, and psychics filtered in to claim their cons. Then my parents emerged, smiling widely.

They were no longer the stress-ridden people who sat nervously in the courtroom years before. Under the tutelage of a Tibetan monk, my mom had developed inner peace about my situation, and my dad . . . well, my dad got food poisoning before the Tibet trip, so he remained a Guinness-swigging Irishman with no affinity for lotus flowers. But he seemed to be doing fine.

"Hey, pumpkin!" My mother's heavy arms engulfed me.

My dad snuck behind her and kissed my forehead. "Hello, love."

I sighed in relief. No matter how old I was, being with my parents always felt like coming home. "Welcome back."

"Thanks, hon." My mom tucked a flyaway hair behind my ear. "After we got done helping your cousin Leslie with the baby, we couldn't help but explore while we were out there. Colorado is so breathtaking that a month went by before we knew it!"

"Retirement." I smiled. "That's the life."

"It really is. Since then, I've been baking up a storm for the church potluck. I'm making your dad taste test everything."

My dad patted his stomach. "I'm not complainin'."

"Rusty's not complaining either, since your father has been feeding him, even though I've repeatedly told him not to!"

Rusty, their seven-year-old Golden Retriever, was the quintessential obedience school dropout, and to my mom's dismay, my dad was a textbook enabler.

"It's not my fault that neither man nor beast can resist your cooking. You're going to blow the rest of those potluck dishes out of the water, love."

"I *am* on my cooking game this year," she admitted. "Harriet Wagner's macaroni salad will eat my dust." She stopped herself and chuckled. "Just kidding."

She was NOT kidding. There is always a cutthroat competition, unspoken and ruthless, between church-going ladies. One breastfeeds while the other is desert dry. One woman's job pays well while the other stays at home with the kids because it's "so rewarding." When push comes to shove, they'll pass toilet paper under the stall, but even then, there is hatred.

"Anyhoo, how's Gregory?"

Oh, Mom. Attempting to be nonchalant about Greg, good try. She asked this question every time I saw her, and it was code for: *When will you and Greg finally get together? I want grandbabies!*

I knew how to handle this: underwhelm her. "He's Greg. Doing the janitor thing."

"That's all?" She frowned. "Nothing new at all?"

"Nope."

"Anything happening between you two yet?" she asked impatiently.

"Nope."

"But he's such a sweet boy."

My mother adored Greg. Unfortunately for her, she was married and thirty years too old for him. Hence she tried to vicariously date him through me. It didn't seem to concern her that I wasn't interested in him.

"I know Greg is nice, Mom. That's why we are *friends*."

"Florence, don't be difficult. Give him a chance."

My father harrumphed. He liked Greg, but preferred my mother not play matchmaker.

She tapped my arm. "You never know, hon."

It always baffled me when my mom used the "You never know" adage. Like really? You never know? What about Hitler? Or Stalin? Bill Cosby? Yeahhhh, sometimes I think ya know.

"Well, I'm not in a place to date someone."

"Damn right!" My father jumped in, unable to hold his tongue any longer. "You are in no position to enter into anything. You need to get your life together."

I ground my teeth.

Reiterating what your kid says—only with an authoritative tone—is a torturous habit all parents pick up at some point. It's an obnoxious practice second only to giving warnings like "don't nail-gun your foot to the floor" or "don't date someone with long fingernails and Velcro shoes." WE KNOW. Calm down.

With that said, parents are the most underappreciated people group on Earth. You pour your time, love, energy, and money into a Baby Clone whose every orifice emits vile substances. Then, as it gets older, it rebels and claims you never gave a damn about it anyways. Eventually the dust settles, but only in time for it to change your adult underwear . . . which it won't because it's a post-modern me-demon busy pursuing its art.

"Not to take the focus off my nonexistent love life, but I've got some good news." The words felt strange on my tongue.

"What is it?" my mom asked apprehensively.

"I, um, I got into the Rehabilitation Seminars."

My mom let out a scream.

"Ssshhh," I looked around at the guards. "It's not official I'm getting out. The Release Board has to approve me. It's not a sure thing."

"Oh please, they're gunna approve you if they're letting you into the Seminars. My baby is getting out in a year!"

"Ten months actually!" I exclaimed.

"I thought it was a yearlong program?"

"It is. It started in June—"

"JUNE?!"

Uh-oh.

"You've known about it for two months?" My mother's eyes brimmed with angry tears. "And you are just telling us now?"

"I wanted to tell you in person," I said, a little defensively. "I didn't know you'd be out of town until the end of summer!"

"Sweetie pie, we were traveling! You can't expect us to twiddle our thumbs at home just because we're retired."

"Mom, I don't expect that! All I'm saying is that I wanted to celebrate with you in person. It's a big deal, and I didn't want to do it over the phone."

"Well, next time a phone call would be nice."

"All right, Mom, next time I evade serious prison time, I will let you know right away."

"Thank you. That's all I ask."

"Congratulations, sweetheart." My dad leaned across the table, kissing my cheek with his prickly mustache. This reaction may seem anti-climatic, but I could feel the joy radiating from his emotionally stunted Irish soul.

"Yes, honey," my mother said, wiping tears from her eyes, "Congratulations!" She came around the table and squeezed me. "My baby girl is coming home."

"MA'AM!" Officer Ramsey yelled. "You need to stay on your side of the table. If I see it again, I will take away her visitation privileges for the next three months. DON'T test me."

It's worth noting that the "no touching" rule was a joke. The only ones who enforced it were Ramsey, the Warden, and the new guards but only when they were in a bad mood. For the most part, guards allowed hand holding, hugging, and even kissing as long as it was PG.

"Of course." She nodded reverently and returned to her seat. Once he wasn't looking, she glared at him. "Hush up, I can hug my girl when she gives me the best news a mother can hear."

"He's a dickhead."

"Language!" she hissed.

"Sorry."

She sighed with relief. "Wow, I'm still in shock. That is so wonderful. I mean, I stopped asking you about the Rehabilitation Seminars a while back because I knew how upset you got when you didn't get chosen."

"Well, luckily I didn't get passed over this time."

"I know, but every year you'd get your hopes up, and every year—"

"Mom. Let's try to keep a positive spin on things, k?"

"Okay, yes! You are getting out!" She crossed her arms on the tabletop, scooted forward, and whispered, "So what are Seminars? There was always so much secrecy."

I knew I wasn't supposed to tell anyone about Decaf, but they were my parents, not sleazy prisoners looking to cheat the system or leak classified information to other inmates. They were just my good, law-abiding, supportive parents. Plus, I was relatively certain that if I *didn't tell* them, my mom would lop off my head—you don't keep secrets in my family. "You cannot repeat what I'm about to tell you to anyone," I whispered. "I'm serious. If anyone finds out I told you, I will go to prison for a *long* time. So you can't tell any aunts, uncles, cousins, people at church, no one. Just nod if you understand."

They both nodded slowly.

I looked around and leaned in closer. "Essentially, I go on a blind date once a week."

"What did I JUST say about you dating in your condition?" my dad bellowed as his short Irish wick burned fiery hot.

"Really, Dad? My condition? I'm not pregnant, and I don't have lupus, so let's cut that out. Plus, they aren't really dates. They're just weird guys the state lined up for us to get to know.

The last two spoke Pig Latin at some point during the Seminar. Trust me, it's a test of patience more than anything."

My dad leaned back. "As long as we're on the same page. No dating."

I nodded. "Love's for the birds."

All of a sudden, Hot-Rod Kim stood up, and all dialogue, internal and external, ceased. A young Smee with an eye patch and full beard had entered from the visitors' side. Every eye was transfixed as Hot-Rod Kim's pirate paramour jubilantly wrapped her up in a hug, burying his smiling face in her burnt-orange hair.

And like a contagious disease, that smile spread from his face to hers.

Her thin lips became a soft pink curve. The bridge of her nose, once a smooth plane marked by nothing, not even a freckle, scrunched into tiny hills. Her blushed round cheeks pushed so high her eyes sparkled like flint hitting stone. If love was for the birds, they were . . . like . . . the proudest, baldest eagles I'd ever seen.

Everyone in the room, including Officer Ramsey, was frozen, mesmerized by their moment. You could hear a pin drop. That is, until the prison-side gate screeched open, and Greg's yelling broke the enchantment. "Two cents for your two cents, good sir?"

My dad perked up. "Is someone willing to pay me a dime for my paradigm?"

"Depends on if you have good news," Greg said with a grin.

"No news is good news."

"Truer words never spoken. Good to see you again, sir." Greg shook my father's hand. "How are you, Carol?"

"I'm a happy camper," Mom answered, hugging him, "now that Florence told us that she'll be home soon."

"You JUST told them?" He whacked my arm with the back of his hand. "You've known for weeks!"

"Thank you! See, Florence, Gregory would have told his mother right away."

"With a dozen roses in hand." He shot my mom the most charming smile I'd ever seen him muster.

Mom threw her hand over her heart. "Did you hear that, Florence? With a dozen roses in hand!"

"I heard it."

"You are such a sweetheart, Gregory. How have you been? You look well."

MOM, GET A ROOM.

"I'm great." He sat down beside me and poked me in the ribs. "Just been trying to keep this one in line."

"We'll have you over for dinner when Florence is home. I'll whip up some lasagna, or maybe I'll splurge on steak. Does that sound good to you, honey? Or do you want some of my lime chicken quesadillas?"

Instantly, my chest felt funny. HEART ATTACK! Wait, no, it wasn't a heart attack. It was different. I tried to gauge the feeling . . . was it sadness again? No, it wasn't sadness or even anger . . . WAIT, WAS THIS HOPE? WAS I ACTUALLY LOOKING FORWARD TO THE FUTURE?

As this new freedom flooded my soul, I imagined my life on the outside. It had been years since I had considered it a possibility; it felt surreal. If the Release Board gave me the thumbs up, I would actually have a future.

Sure, I would be unemployed with a criminal record and no recent job history, but I'd be free. Free to go to all the obligations that people took for granted: graduation parties, gynecology appointments, the DMV. I couldn't wait to immerse myself in everyday life again. Normalcy was an overlooked pleasure, and I was going to soak up every moment. I just had to get through the next ten months.

CHAPTER 20

Jonathan

The Open Door's "Specials" insert was taunting me with two mouth-watering options, and I was trapped in a full-out food conundrum. How was I going to choose between coconut-crusted shrimp and strip steak? Forcing me to pick favorites seemed needlessly cruel, but due to the oppressive "one meal per Seminar" rule, I had to choose. And the decision was becoming increasingly impossible by the minute . . . because I COULD NOT HEAR MYSELF THINK.

For some God-forsaken reason, the waiter clearing the table next to me was frantically chucking plates and silverware into a busser's bin. Judging by the sound of smashing, The Open Door was losing some prime dish inventory. The waiter sprinted between abandoned tables, cleaning them at lightning speed. I didn't know where the fire was, but he was going to be the first one on the scene. He raced into the kitchen, the door swinging in his wake.

Now that he was gone, it was time to seriously weigh my options: the pride of the sea with mango chutney or a true bovine beauty leaking luscious moo juices. This was my Sophie's choice. This was the moment that I proved what kind of woman I was.

Suddenly, the table jolted, and the frazzled waiter materialized in the chair across from me.

"Hey." He quickly ran his fingers through his disheveled hair and took off his nametag. "I'm—"

"Excuse me!" Officer Ramsey stampeded across the restaurant. "You need special clearance to sit there." He yanked the waiter out of his seat by the elbow. "It's for your safety."

"If you let me go, I'll show you my clearance."

Officer Ramsey's Tom-Selleck moustache twitched with aggravation. He reluctantly released the waiter, who dug a wallet out of his back pocket and whipped out a folded pink piece of paper.

"You should've given this to us first!"

"Sorry." The waiter shrugged.

"Can't be too careful with this population." Officer Ramsey said, hiking up his pants by his belt.

"I appreciate the valor you've exhibited in protecting me from her."

Officer Ramsey glared. You could see those Neanderthal gears turning, trying to figure out whether this waiter was sassing him or respecting him. It took a few seconds for him to give up, mumble something about his civic duty, and slink back to his table.

The waiter offered his hand. "Sorry about that. Let's start over. I'm Jonathan."

"Florence." I shook his hand. "You work here?"

"I do."

"Why?"

He sighed. "It's sort of a filler job until I find one that uses my degree or—"

"No, sorry," I interrupted, "I meant, why did you sign up for the Rehabilitation Seminars?"

Between lecturing us on fart-dampening techniques and proper posture, Dr. Sean had explained The Open Door's collaboration with Coffee. The restaurant was run by a liver-spotted social worker with a 401k to spare. He opened his doors to AA, NA, Al-Anon, and Coffee Correctional Facility's Rehabilitation Seminars; therefore, every employee was thoroughly warned about the establishment's rabble-rousing patrons and the risks of working among them. So if this Jonathan enrolled in Decaf, knowing what he knew, it was a red flag. Plus he was relatively attractive, so again, why was he here?

"You want to know why I signed up for the Rehab Seminars." He pondered this for a moment. "How do I put this without sounding creepy?"

Perfect start.

"Is it a fetish thing?" I asked apprehensively. Rumor had it we had a couple handcuff fetishists in our midst.

"Admittedly," he said, biting his lip, "I was hoping you'd be in uniform. I've always loved those black and white stripes."

Aaaaand there it was.

"Sorry to disappoint." I picked up the menu, blocking his gaze. If this guy was going to spend the whole night fantasizing about me in an old-timey prison uniform, I deserved the surf and turf combo.

"I'm kidding," he said, pulling down my menu and smirking like a Keebler elf. "I work here, so even if I did have a jumpsuit fetish, WHICH I DON'T, I know you guys wear normal clothes."

"Okay. Then, the question remains: Why did you sign up for the Seminars?"

"The truth is, I've seen you around, and you seemed cool, so I wanted to have dinner with you." A grin teased the edges of his mouth. "Plus, who can resist an evening with a beautiful woman?"

This guy was an idiot.

"You're an idiot."

He laughed. "Why?"

"You volunteered to fake date an alleged murderer because you thought I seemed cool? Didn't anyone ever teach you Stranger Danger?"

He squinted. "You said alleged."

"What?"

"You said you are an alleged murderer."

"Yeah?"

"Being an alleged murderer is different than being an actual murderer."

I could see where this was going.

"So are you an alleged murderer or an actual murderer?"

I learned early on that these conversations were a terrible use of my time. People either got off on hearing my wrongfully imprisoned tale or thought I was lying. But even though I didn't want to come off as crazy, I wasn't going to admit to something I didn't do.

"Alleged," I conceded.

"So you've never killed anyone?"

"No, but I'm not here to convince you. I'm here to eat food and prove that I can be civil with the opposite sex."

"No convincing needed. I believe you're innocent."

"Oh yeah," I said, putting down my menu, "and why is that? Because I seem *so* cool?"

"No, because I've waited on my fair share of inmates, and you don't seem like the murdering type," he said plainly.

Our waitress hopped in front of our table with long, agile strides. She had always reminded me of a gazelle with her flowing brown ponytail and sharp facial features. Normally, she was strictly business, but tonight she wore a giddy smile. "Hey, Jonathan."

"Hey, Bekah," he said. "This is Florence. Florence, Bekah."

"I've seen ya around."

I smiled nervously. Bekah had been my waitress since day one, and I could only imagine what she overheard while refilling our drinks. I prayed she hadn't witnessed the worst of it.

"How are your Seminars going?" she asked, tightening her pony/gazelle tail.

"They're okay," I said, with a touch of relief. She was probably too busy to pay attention to the carnage of my Seminars.

"I don't know if you know this, but one of the guys cut a piece of your hair off." She traced her slender finger in the air. "It wasn't the guy who cried, but a few weeks before that."

"Ah, you noticed that too?"

"Don't worry, this guy won't give you any haircuts." She blocked her mouth with the back of her hand and whispered, "He's been looking forward to this all week."

"All riiiight, all right." Jonathan reddened almost imperceptibly. "How about you get us those waters?"

Bekah grinned deviously. "Don't let him bore you with his social policy rants."

"Who doesn't love debating healthcare legislation?" he asked.

"Everyone," Bekah called over her shoulder. "Be right back with your waters."

"You should try the breakfast for dinner," Jonathan suggested. "It's not on the menu, but it's incredible."

And that was it. There was no more talk of murder, alleged or otherwise. Whether he believed me or had extreme ADD, I didn't know, but either way, this was turning out to be one of the better dinners I'd ever had.

I ended up taking him up on his breakfast-for-dinner suggestion. People who work in a restaurant know all its secret treasures, and I knew I'd be remiss if I didn't heed his advice. I was not disappointed. Imagine piles of supple pancakes littered with sweet blueberries, with syrup thick as molasses dripping off of the fluffy, delicate stacks. Now imagine crunchy, brown hash browns seasoned with just enough Cajun seasoning to blow your mind and bacon so delectable, the pigs must have been raised behind the pearly gates (grazing on grass and angel kisses). It was enough to make you fertile.

But it wasn't just the delicious pancakes and accoutrements that were unexpected. It was Jonathan. For being slightly hot, he was surprisingly funny. He must have been fat when he was young. He had that witty, self-deprecating humor characteristic of fat kids: the kind that is neither cruel nor isolating because it was cultivated by insecurity and overcompensation. Its disarming quality caught me off guard—and caused me to choke on my pancakes.

"Stop, stop," I laugh-coughed.

"Sorry. Here, drink." He pushed my water toward me.

"If I die by pancake"—I coughed, taking a sip—"I'm fine with it, but make sure that I'm buried in a coffin full of these pancakes."

"Even if they're the cause of death?"

"Yes." I nodded, taking another sip. "Promise me."

"Eh, I can't promise that."

"Jonathan," I warned between coughs. "It's my dying wish."

"I'll try, but if I end up eating them on the way to the funeral"—he stole a piece of pancake off my plate—"you can't haunt me."

"If you keep that up," I said, scowling as he went for another piece of pancake, "I will haunt you, and your children, and your children's children."

"For the amount of time that my laptop has spent on my lap, I doubt I can have kids any time soon. It's probably like Chernobyl down there."

With lightning-fast speed, he stabbed another piece of pancake and shoved it into his mouth.

"Dude!" I exclaimed. "I'm officially haunting you."

"Okay, but you're going to see some weird stuff." He laughed, pushing up his sleeves. I was surprised to see that his left forearm was covered in a graffiti ocean of deep blues and purples. The ink cascaded over his slightly protruding veins, ending just below his elbow. A half-sleeve. Surprisingly, no busty American flag-toting mermaid swam majestically through the tattooed waters. HELLS YEAH, give me some of that non-frat tat.

Historically, I was drawn to a very specific type of guy. By my early twenties, it was deeply formulaic: Coca-Cola colored hair, eyes with sunken brows, and reserved smiles. And a little meat on his bones never hurt.

Jonathan was the opposite of all that. He was an Aryan wet dream with windswept blonde hair, blue irises that expanded in excitement when we had something in common, and a dimple that dipped deep into his right cheek. Not to mention, I easily outweighed him by fifteen pounds. He wasn't mysterious, and he hadn't once mentioned the complications of modern morality. Not my type at all.

However, there was something about him that was easy. It drew me in and made me feel like I could kick off my heels and relax. Maybe it was his humor, maybe it was the purity of his Icelandic looks, or maybe it was the fact that he could talk menstruation.

MENSTRUATION? WHAAA?

Okay, calm your tee tahs. I didn't discuss my duration or flow viscosity; I have *some* discretion. But debilitating cramps did come up, and he did not melt into a pile of erotophobic goo. I was impressed.

How a man handled the hurricane in my vajayjay had always been a litmus test for my romantic relationships. If, in the throes of my uterine battle, a guy was willing to buy me tampons without a fuss, he had proven that he could step up. But if he passed out at the thought of a maxi-pad, he had proven that I was dating a child, and since I'm not a pedophile, that was a deal breaker.

So for Jonathan to touch on the topic without a visceral reaction of "COOTIES" was pretty sexy. This sexiness made more sense when I found out he had a sister. Guys with sisters always have thicker skin about placentas and such.

"My sister Jen and I used to fight all the time. When I was ten, I cussed at Jen, and I got in HUGE trouble. And the insult didn't even make sense! I said something like 'you are so pissing stupid.'"

"That sounds British."

"I know! It was the first time I ever said a 'bad word,' and when my mom heard, she made me sit with soap in my mouth like in *The Christmas Story*. I kind of looked like Ralphie actually. Had the glasses and everything."

Former fat kid: check.

"Your mom was pretty strict then?"

"Nah, she was reasonable. We didn't have a lot of rules, but she enforced the ones we had. I think I got grounded six times total."

"What about your dad?" I asked. The light drained from Jonathan's eyes. "Sorry, it's none of my business."

"No, that's okay." He heaved a small breath. "He abused me when I was little. When my mom found out, she beat the hell out him, filed charges, and divorced him. He was in jail for a while, but now he's living somewhere in Arizona."

My foot was shoved so far into my mouth that there were teeth marks in my soles. "I'm sorry."

"You didn't know," he replied graciously. "My dad was selfish and reckless, but my mom made up for it. She was and is the strongest person I know. She managed to raise Jen and me with an impressive amount of ease. I think she saw what she had to do and just did it."

Mental note: Get on his mom's good side. Also, get more pancakes.

The night continued on with lighter notes of blonde jokes and favorite pastimes, ending as our dinners noisily rumbled their ways through our digestive tracks. It was a curiously lovely evening.

CHAPTER 21

Earth

Throughout the week, I looked back on my time with Jonathan with a touch of exhilaration. Prisoner or not, it was nice to have a handsome guy interested in spending an evening with me.

Unfortunately, at 6:17 p.m. the following Friday, my week-long whimsy was dashed as I violently crashed down to Earth. Literally. After vehemently apologizing for tripping and falling into my beatnik date's lap, I sat across from Earth.

"Sorry we kept you waiting," Officer Ramsey said politely. "Terrible traffic. Drove as fast as we could."

With a twinkle in his stoner eye, Earth responded with, "Time is a social construct, man, so it doesn't even matter."

Officer Ramsey's one-time departure from douchebaggery had been wasted on a man who wasn't wearing shoes, but who *was* wearing eleven ankle bracelets. Sorry, bro.

For the rest of the night, Earth—dreadlocked flower child of mother Gaia—proclaimed passionate tidbits like:

- "I want to meet all the colors on the canvas of life!"

- "A low income is no excuse for eating white bread!"

- "Capitalism!"

- "Greed!"
- "Legalization!"

He was baaaaaaaked.

Eventually, Bekah brought out Earth's bean-sprout wrap and my vindictively ordered chef salad. It was the dirtiest meat mash I'd ever seen, with extra-greasy bacon overflowing the edges of the bowl. Earth's Adam's apple bobbed in disgust, and I was satisfied before the first bite.

About midway through dinner, Jonathan sauntered into my peripheral vision. Immediately, I became entranced with Earth McDirtyHippy. In the sciences, this defense mechanism is referred to as "Awkward Avoidance,"[13] and it'd been a while since I had this reaction. He was just a friendly guy I shared one meal with, nothing to get flustered about.

Nonetheless, I was so deft at the art of avoidance that, by the time Earth pulled out a wad of bark and left for the bathroom, I had half-forgotten Jonathan existed.

Seated by the windows were two groups of Parrot Heads sporting leis and tie-dye shirts that read, "It's five o'clock somewhere." I could almost see the alcohol evaporating off of them; one strike of a match, and this whole place would be obliterated.

Jimmy Buffet, you chill genius, bringing people together once again.

---

13 Awkward Avoidance (\'ɔ kwərd ə'vɔɪd əns\): a reaction most commonly associated with self-respecting women who avoid eye contact with someone they'd like to paint like one of their French girls.

In college, my friends and I had road-tripped to a Buffet concert. The pre-game was filled with inflatable pools, keg stands, margaritas, and spinning wheels with options like "Show Your Ta-Tas" and "Take a Shot." It was spring break with no age limit. Middle-aged women with sunburnt noses and old men with hairy chests hitting each other with water balloons and eating salt 'n' vinegar chips. It was a Bohemian mad house, and I loved it. I'm happy to say that I almost made it through the concert without throwing up! Almost. But you can't be dizzy-drunk and hear "cheeseburger in paradise" without consequences. Margaritaville: where everyone belonged and everyone was drunk.

"Hi!" a voice boomed.

My heart knocked hard against my ribs.

Jonathan was standing beside me, looking concerned. "Sorry, I didn't mean to scare you. I just wanted to say goodbye before I left."

"Why?" I asked, trying to clear my head of cheeseburgers and paradise.

He looked confused.

"I mean, why are you leaving during the dinner rush?" *Smooth, Florence.*

"My grad school applications are due at the end of this week, and my manager's letting me go home to work on them. I'm a slow writer."

"How many programs are you applying to?"

"Four. My first choice is Andersen-Williams because it's close and has the highest reviews. The other three are back-ups; two of them are online programs."

A sliver of me was happy to hear that Jonathan was staying around. NOT FOR ANY SENTIMENTAL REASON, but because the community could use someone like Jonathan. You know, because he was passionate about healthcare reform and its impact and stuff. Yup, good for the community.

"I used the same essay for all my undergrad applications. They all ask the same thing— how are you going to contribute to the university and/or society? I don't know about you, but I'm definitely contributing to society right now." I motioned to the prison guards at the next table.

"I'm twenty k in debt working at a restaurant that is rated three stars on Yelp, so"—he huffed on his nails and wiped them on his shirt—"I'm killing it too."

"Well, go home and demolish those essays. Put on some music, have a snack, and keep a cyanide capsule on hand just in case."

"That's graduate-level thinking." He grinned. "See you next week?"

"I'll be here."

My energy levels diminished quickly as my Jonathan-induced hormone surge waned. I did what I could to stay awake, but Earth's diatribe about the Styrofoam Cup Crisis was a real buzzkill. I tried pinching myself, reciting the alphabet backward, and counting the ceiling tiles, but nothing was working.

I eventually resorted to pushing my bowl slightly to the left. Then slightly to the right. Then slightly away from me. Then slightly toward me.

It was not an exciting life, but it was mine.

About three-fourths of the way through Earth's Reggae Appreciation, something sliced the tip of my right finger. Retracting my hand, I found a thin line dividing my fingerprint, increasingly engorged with blood. I examined my bowl for broken glass and found a miniscule white triangle jutting out beneath it. With my un-maimed fingers, I tweezed the white triangle. It became a small square of folded paper with "Florence" written in Unabomber handwriting. Throat tensed, I tried to slip it into my pocket, only to find that the pocket was sewn shut. I tried the other three pockets, but they were sewn up too. *Makes sense. It's faster to frisk prisoners when they don't have pockets full of contraband.*

Nympho Yvette would know what to do. She was the resident smuggler, always sneaking in cigarettes, quality tampons, and *Playgirl* magazines. She did take special orders, but she had to be careful about it because if the guards searched the cells and found what they considered "significant contraband" (cell phones, weapons, healing crystals), we were subjected to a cavity search. As if someone can even fit a healing crystal up their . . . orifices. *(Shudders violently.)*

I had never smuggled anything before, but I knew I had to be smart about it. If I got caught, that'd be the final nail in my coffin. Dr. Sean might have been able to overlook an outburst or two (*cough* Vincent *cough*), but to get caught sneaking something in from a Seminar would be too much for him to excuse. I had to be strategic.

The average frisking at Coffee started with the guards checking our shoes, then doing a quick once-over with the backs of their hands. It ended with them checking the insides of our mouths.[14] And like I said, even though they only did cavity searches on very special occasions, I didn't want to shove the note up any of my . . . orifices. *(Shudders violently.)*

Then I had an idea so inspired that I couldn't believe it had taken me this long to come up with it. Subtly, I took the note from under my leg and pretended to itch my head. Then I slipped it into my messy, curly bun. I felt my disobedient, mind-of-its-own hair engulfing the note, causing it to disappear completely.

And there it stayed, in the jungle atop my head, until I returned to Coffee.

---

14 In case we tried to smuggle acorns in our big ol' chipmunk cheeks.

CHAPTER 22

Someone's in Love . . .

Gingerly, I set the note on my bed. I gazed upon its crisp edges, cherishing the small, folded paper square. Tenderly, I placed it under my pillow. Whatever the letter said would read sweeter in the soft morning light. It was worth the wait.

HAHA JK. Delayed gratification is for people who didn't grow up in America. I ripped that sucker open.

You look nice tonight.
–J

Four words. Four words was all it took to fill my stomach with butterflies—atrocious pterodactyl butterflies with serrated metal wings, but butterflies nevertheless.

No one had passed me a note since high school, and even though I felt juvenile and stupid, there was something old-school romantic about it. Plus when you'd spent the last five years without a heart flutter, this kind of thing was exciting.

I wanted to tell someone, but I had to choose wisely.

Feminist Lorraine would tell me how men ruin women, and Nympho Yvette would encourage me to try butt stuff. Lovely Elizabeth was an option, but knowing her, she might prefer to be left in the dark. My getting involved with a Decaf date was probably against the rules, and she might be considered guilty by association. So I settled on Susie the Strangler. Her non-gossipy, maternal nature made her the perfect candidate for my girlish outpouring.

The bigger question was when to approach her. The following day was Saturday, which meant that the morning would be split between Expressive Dance Therapy and Arts and Crafts. Neither was private enough to have an actual conversation, so I'd have to wait until the afternoon, intercept her in the courtyard.

But on Saturday, before going into the courtyard, we were subjected to a glorious cavity search! Apparently, Nympho Yvette had decided to smuggle in a giant lime-green dildo—and hid it under her pillow, which is total amateur hour. Hide your dildos better, Nympho Yvette!

I had almost shaken off the violated-sock-puppet feeling by the time we shuffled single file into the courtyard. The guards shut the door behind us and unlocked our cuffs. I was the caboose, and Susie the Strangler was somewhere near the front of the line. I rose to my tiptoes to see over other the inmates when, suddenly, Nympho Yvette grabbed my wrist. "Come here!"

"Not today, Yvette. I need to talk to Susie about something."

But Nympho Yvette wasn't listening. She lugged me through the assorted prisoners. The crisp autumn leaves crunched under my feet as I tried to keep up.

Nympho Yvette grabbed Yosemite Karen's arm. She scowled, but came along reluctantly.

"Susie! Elizabeth! Follow me," Nympho Yvette hissed as she dragged us along.

"Y'all playing Red Rover?" Susie the Strangler asked.

"I have to tell you all something," Nympho Yvette said, motioning her over to the corner of the courtyard. From here, you could see the chemical plant's smokestacks vomiting synthetic clouds. The metallic aroma wasn't completely unpleasant, but it was, slowly but surely, giving us pre-cancer.[15]

Susie the Strangler put her hands over her eyes and shook her head. "Tell me you aren't giving yourself another tattoo."

"No, Mom," Nympho Yvette huffed. "Dr. Sean said if I tatted myself again, he'd advise against my release. He says it's part of my 'pattern of addiction.'"

She rolled her eyes as if she'd never heard anything so absurd. As if her leapfrogging from conquest to conquest had nothing to do with the dozens of meaningless tattoos covering her tiny, sturdy frame. She looked like a comic book antagonist with her thick, wavy black hair and inked-up skin. She was only missing the leather boots and the BMI required for giant boobs.

"Your future employers will thank you," Susie the Strangler said.

"I barely have room left for more tattoos anyways. Except for my thighs. But those are always open."

---

15 Like Febreze and microwaves.

"HA!" Yosemite Karen laughed. "Good one."

"Oh my gosh! Just tell us what you need to tell us!" I said. She was taking up the very limited time I had to tell Susie about Jonathan's note.

"Fine, Miss Impatient. Here goes." She paused dramatically. "I am in love!"

"You've got to be kidding me." Stupid-jerkface-horndog, taking the glory away from my thing . . .

"You're not in love." Yosemite Karen shook Nympho Yvette's grip from her wrist.

"I am! We've already gone on a date." She grinned. "Your tax dollars at work."

"He was one of the guys from the blind dates?" Yosemite Karen whispered.

My stomach dropped. "You're not in Decaf. Who told you?"

"Like Yvette could keep that a secret?"

Lovely Elizabeth gasped. "Yvette! You've put us all at risk! How could you?"

"She was bugging me. It's fine; she isn't going to tell anyone."

Truthfully, I didn't like Yosemite Karen. She was a bully, and I didn't trust her as far as I could throw her.[16]

"If they find out that you know, we could all get kicked out," I said.

---

16 Which wasn't far—she was built like an armored truck.

"I'm not going to tell anyone." Yosemite Karen rolled her eyes. "Now shut up. I want to hear more about the guy who's trolling Decaf for a girlfriend. What's his name?"

"Fr-r-r-rancesco," Nympho Yvette purred.

"Francesco?" Yosemite Karen repeated. "Clearly, a skeeze-ball."

"If anything, he's an otherworldly sex god. Like Thor. But with a bigger dick." She bit her lip in elation. "His hands were like a mammogram!"[17]

"Are you claiming that you bedded him while the guards were on watch?"

"Don't be crass, Elizabeth!" Nympho Yvette said. "I don't have sex with everyone I meet!"

"Oh!" she yelped. "I didn—I shouldn't have—"

"Kidding, we banged in the bathroom."

"And you didn't get caught?" I asked.

"No, and I don't know how they didn't see it coming. We played footsy so hard I broke a nail."

(Commence internal vomiting.)

"He's a predator," Yosemite Karen said.

"Not Francesco. He's yummy like candy."

Yosemite Karen guffawed. "Which predators use to lure children into their vans!"

"If he had sex with Yvette, he's probably not into children," Susie the Strangler said.

---

17 For any man out there whose girlfriend is making you read this book: There is nothing erotic about a booby tourniquet, so BE GENTLE! Unless your ladylove is into S&M. In that case, wrench away!

Nympho Yvette ignored them, whirling like a starry-eyed Dervish. "The sex was unmatched. His hands were warm like butter, and he went down like a coal miner."[18]

"You don't need a man to get sexual pleasure!" Feminist Lorraine emerged out of nowhere. "There are plenty of personal pleasure devices you can use instead to achieve the same effects."

"I'm no stranger to the dildo, Lorraine. I just got busted with one, remember? I'm not talking about pleasure. I'm talking about love."

"If there's anyone you should preach to about dildos, it's Abigail," Susie the Strangler said. "She needs one. I think she's starting to direct all her pent-up sexual energy at Officer Carmel."

"I've heard their exchanges. They get . . ." Lovely Elizabeth gulped. "Graphic."

"Guys, focus," Yosemite Karen said. "Yvette, you do know that only weirdos volunteer to meet women like us, right? Normal guys make a Tinder account or go to bars."

"Most of those Tinder guys aren't the cream of the crop either," Susie the Strangler said. "I've heard a concernin' number of them are into spankin'."

"Hallelujah," Nympho Yvette sang.

---

18 Nympho Yvette spoke about her exploits in tangled, convoluted metaphors for which I was always grateful. It kept me from visualizing anything unsavory.

"You're not listening," Yosemite Karen said. "He's too shady for Tinder; he has to resort to Decaf to get laid."

"Hold on now." Susie the Strangler put up her hands. "He could be the exception to the Weirdo Rule."

Lovely Elizabeth averted her eyes. "You must admit it's *unusual* to say the least."

But Nympho Yvette wasn't listening. She was riding a high that no one could touch.

I, on the other hand, was ready to deny my Decaf crush at the rooster's crow. My joy-turned-shame could only be likened to giving birth to a beautiful baby, then realizing you pooped on the table.

I'd had about all I could stomach, so I explored the courtyard alone. Autumn was beautiful in Maine, incarcerated or not. We were surrounded by pine trees which stood their deep-green ground, but there were small clusters of normal trees (maple, oak, something or other) that shed their multicolored leaves into the courtyard. I wished I could climb their emptying branches and camp out there forever. But winter would be on its way soon enough with snow banks, blizzards, and freezing-cold temperatures that could numb an Eskimo's testicle.

I was so caught up in my thoughts that I didn't even notice Greg until his lanky frame slammed into my side. "Oh, sorry, ma'am."

I struggled to regain my balance. "Don't you ever work?"

"What's your problem, Grumpy Pants?"

"Nothing." I didn't want to talk about Jonathan or Francesco or Eskimo testicles.

"Walk with me," he said, linking my arm with his. "Why so serious, Batman?"

"I'm fine."

"I know what's bothering you." He moved a strand of hair out of my face. "Now that you're in the Seminars, it's finally hitting you that your days are numbered here, and you're nervous that you'll lose touch with everyone."

"Um, not sure where you're getting that from." I returned the strand of hair to my face. "I'm VERY much looking forward to losing touch with everyone here."

"Yeah, right."

I looked at him seriously.

"Oh." His voice cracked. "Not me though, right? Because I'm not even part of this whole thing! We met here, but that's it! I'm not going to remind you of this place after you're out!"

"Chill. I wasn't talking about you. We'll hang out after; don't worry." I smiled. "We'll actually have to coordinate work schedules."

"Are you looking forward to working?" Greg asked, eyes wide in disbelief.

"That and Starbucks."

"You're weird." He laughed, leaning against me. "Where are you even gunna work?"

"I have a degree in early childhood development," I said, "so I'm going to go back to childcare like before."

Greg shot me a sideways glance. "With your record?"

"It'll be tough," I agreed hesitantly, "but if worse comes to worse, I can do private nannying."

"No parent is going to hire you. Ever heard of a background check?"

"Thanks for the confidence boost, friend." I frowned, and released his arm.

"Flo, I wasn't—"

I ignored him and headed to the basketball court. The Domestics and First Lady Abigail were lying on the sidelines, tuckered out from their last game. I wedged the vintage blue-and-red basketball from between the legs of the courtside bench and bounced it as high as it would go.

Greg was wrong. The best kinds of nannies are the ones who have murder raps.

Clean up, clean up! Everybody, everywhere!
Clean up, clean up! Or I'll choke you with your hair!

I took a free-throw shot; the ball teased the edges of the metal basket before falling anticlimactically off the side of the hoop into a dirt pile.

Fine. Greg was right. I was screwed. The only kind of family who'd want a murderer watching their kids was the kind whose kids slept in cages, not bunk beds, and as much as I thought kids should eat their vegetables, I wasn't going to hook the little guys up to a car battery if they didn't clear their plates.

Maybe I could pioneer the untapped market of crack-house daycares. I'd be a woman at the forefront of her field, like Madame Curie or Indira Gandhi. I mean, think about it: When is a parent more in need of childcare than when they're scoring rock? Regrettably, crack addicts aren't known for their disposable income, so I'd have to devise a manageable payment plan. Maybe a bartering system. It's what our ancestors did for centuries, before paper money made every exchange impersonal and detached. I was going to be the kind of artisan-crack-house-day-care-director that you could truly connect with.

Crackhouse Care: A Name You Can Trust.

CHAPTER 23

Reminiscing

In light of Nympho Yvette's confession, I decided to keep the Jonathan thing to myself. I had four ounces of pride left, which, liquefied, is more than you are allowed in a carry-on, so I figured it was worth preserving.

Nevertheless, I wrote him a short note, stuffed it into a plastic baggy, and hid the baggy in my government-sanctioned sports bra.[19] With the girls secured and the note beneath them, I was off.

My date stared into my eyes intently, ignoring the half-eaten chicken Alfredo on his plate. "Dude, I swear I know you from somewhere."

"Andrew, we've been doing this for an hour, and thus far we've established that you don't know me from soccer camp, school, or any number of yoga retreats in West Palm Beach. I think it's time to admit that we've never met."

He snapped his fingers. "Did you take surf lessons in Key West?"

"No."

---

19 That was a jailhouse trick I learned from a former prisoner, Rianna, whose boob sweat turned her crisp poker winnings into a sopping wet pile of non-currency.

"Are you sure?"

"Yes. I promise. I've never been to Florida, and it's safe to assume I've never done anything that involves coordination or adrenaline. Or better yet, you can assume that I'm correct in saying that we have never, ever met before."

He stroked his goatee. "No, I'll figure it out."

Suddenly, a high-pitched beeping sounded from under the table. Andrew pulled a small black square out of his cargo pants.

"Is that a pager?"

"Yeah, be right back." He scurried to the door, eyeing the guards nervously.

"What is he?" Jonathan asked, wiping down the table next to me. "A nineties drug dealer?"

I turned my chair toward him. "Yes, sir. That's exactly what he is."

"You two seem chummy. Where do you know him from again?"

"Nowhere! Wait . . . are you messing with me?"

"A little."

I grinned. "Thank goodness, I was about to lose it."

"And that's why there are no knives allowed at your table."[20] He smirked. "You should just tell him that you bought weed off him that one time."

"That's brilliant, actually."

---

20 "No knives at the table" was a dumb rule. If Coffee really thought we were going to stab someone, then they shouldn't approve us for Decaf. Nevertheless, the kitchen cut up our food (and our date's food) for us. Why not go the extra mile and pre-chew our food while they were at it?

He yawned. "That's why they pay me the big bucks."

I noticed dark circles hugging the bottom of his eyes like little crescent moons, and blonde stubble springing up in patches on his face. "You look exhausted."

"I finished my grad school applications earlier today . . . like three a.m. earlier."

"Why didn't you take the day off?"

"We're short-staffed. Half of the kitchen staff has mono, so it's only me, Bekah, and Roy."

Restaurant employees were always incestuous, and when they went down, they went down like dominos.

"I don't think my applications turned out well. At one point I zoned out, and when I came to, I had drawn a dinosaur in Paint."

"Yikes."

"Yeah, I was trying to attach it to my application."

"That's not good."

"No. Maybe it's time I give up and pursue my alternative career path."

"Which is?"

"Stripping," he said nonchalantly. "I could start dieting and working out. Magic Mike myself."

"I don't think that's a viable option for men."

"I disagree; I could make a lucrative career out of it."

"Only if you've got the moves."

"Oh, I have the moves." He smiled seductively. "And I'll let you in on a little secret: people think it's all in the hips, but the trick is the shoulders."

"The shoulders?"

"Oh yes, shoulder moves can be very erotic." He lowered his head and rolled his shoulder in front of his face like a scruffy geisha. "Sometimes I move beyond erotic into a post-erotic dimension, so shield your eyes if it gets to be too much." He made his left shoulder bounce, then his right, like some rigor mortis–stricken marionette.

"That's pre-erotic at best."

He attempted to shimmy. "I'll get there."

"You have no shame."

"There's a pretty good chance that I'll look back on this moment and be mortified."

I laughed, causing the folded note in my sports bra to rub against me. "Oh! I almost forgot!"

I was reaching into my shirt to get the note when suddenly, Andrew burst through Coffee's door, grabbing his poncho hood off his head. "I just realized where I know you from!"

Jonathan and I exchanged grins. "Yeah? And where do you know me from?"

"You were that girl who got charged with killing her boyfriend based on a crazy amount of circumstantial evidence! Right?"

I froze.

"It *is* you! I was in a criminal law class that semester, and my professor loved your case. We followed your trial on TV, like, every class. Oh man, you should have seen my professor's face when you got convicted. He was so pissed."

"I should go," Jonathan said abruptly.

"Could you grab me a Mountain De—"Andrew started, but Jonathan had disappeared in record time. Andrew shrugged, then turned his attention back to me. "It's crazy that I'm meeting you! We even had a mock trial based on yours. I was your fake attorney, and I'm happy to say that I got a not guilty verdict."

"Thanks?"

"I always thought his new girlfriend did it. She was sick hot, but she had the crazy eyes. Like, all the pictures of them together, they look super happy but, like, I also thought that she looked a little murder-y. You know, like, she was suspiciously hot." He pulled on his goatee. "To be honest, I was on 'shrooms once when I was studying for that law class, and I . . . uh . . . cranked down to her picture. But, in my defense, she looked like a hot dragon sorceress because I was tripping balls."

I gaped at him helplessly, too horrified to answer.

"Did you know her? Did you talk to her ever? Do you think she did it?"

"I'm not talking about Her."

Out of nowhere, Officer Carmel came from behind Andrew and put a hand on his shoulder. "Thank you for your participation. Please head over to the table and fill out the evaluation there. After you're done, you are free to leave."

I never liked Officer Carmel, but in that moment, I could've kissed him. Instead, I excused myself to the bathroom, dug the note out of my bra, and threw it in the toilet. The plastic bag adhered to the paper, showcasing my scribbled words. *You don't look so bad yourself.*

I flushed and watched the note swirl and disappear down the drain. It was done. I breathed easier . . . until the baggy reemerged, wrinkled and dirty from the failed trip down. Buoyant bastard. I flushed again and again and again, but it returned more ugly and shit-covered each time.

Symbolic of my last six years.

It hadn't occurred to me that people paid attention to my trial, but in retrospect, the media was all over it.

Everyone loves drama, and my trial was a drama bomb:

- a merciless DA arguing that an innocent accountant was strangled to death for reconnecting with his college sweetheart

- an overconfident public defender claiming that there wasn't a shred of forensic evidence to support the state's case

- and an accused ex-girlfriend (yours truly) whose scarf was the murder weapon.

The prosecution painted a juicy, albeit false, picture with the circumstantial evidence, but I had confidence in the people.

The American justice system was built on fair trials, careful discernment of the truth, and unwavering devotion to justice.

The jurors deliberated for an hour and were home by dinner.

It was the first in a long line of eye-opening experiences in the so-called criminal justice system. Sometimes justice is unjust, and the truth doesn't set you free.

There was a silver lining, however. His name was Judge Rainier. He was my sentencing judge, and a real stickler for DNA evidence. His Honor straight-out said that the jury rushed to judgment, and that though he wouldn't overturn their decision, he could sentence me to a place called Coffee Correctional Facility. I had never heard of it, but if it meant I'd abbreviate my incarceration by twenty-five years, I was thankful. Small mercies, right?

Well, fuck small mercies. I wanted big mercies. I wanted to sleep in a bed that didn't get overturned weekly for contraband checks, I wanted to walk outside without a barbed wire fence cutting through my view, and I wanted to flirt with a sexy server without someone bringing up my g-damn murder conviction.

I understood why Jonathan bolted. I really did. Nice guys can't take the heat, and my life was a convection oven. It was bound to happen sooner or later. So shout-out to Andrew: excellent use of my past to cock-block. Nice preemptive work.

CHAPTER 24

Family Ties

Susie the Strangler's husband kissed her fingers softly, looking up with his tired hazel eyes. He buried his face in her wrist, and breathed her in. The combination of love, sadness, and guilt pouring from Susie the Strangler's eyes was palpable.

He lifted his head and mouthed "I love you." His hands, stained from working on cars, cupped her cheek.

"I love you," she mouthed back.

Years ago, they promised "for better or worse," but I bet Susie the Strangler never thought she'd be the "for worse." Maybe it was best to be alone here. Susie the Strangler's life was a cluster like mine, and her husband's pain was too hard to watch. I couldn't do it. If I were her, I would've had to let him go (or else I'd never sleep again), but they were fueled by love or stubbornness.

"Hey, beautiful," a voice said from behind me.

I turned around. "Good one."

Greg crashed down next to me. "What are you doing here?"

"I have these things called parents. You're probably not familiar with the term, since you were raised by wolves."

"I wish I was raised by wolves."

"Ah, sorry." From what Greg had told me about his parents, they sucked butt. His dad was militant with a tinge of ultra-religious fervor, and his mom was a pill-popping alcoholic. Not exactly the dream team. "Well, I'm here to visit mine."

Greg rapped his knuckled against my head. "Dummy, they're visiting what's-her-name in DC."

Blerg.

He was right. My crazy fertile cousins were popping out kids left and right (which I guess is what happens when you spend your time getting it on instead of rotting in jail), and my parents were making their obligatory rounds to see the little ones. The guards only bring you out when you have a visitor, but they must have been so absorbed in their soon-to-be-retirement dreams that they accidentally brought me without thinking.

"Dang it." I got up. "I guess I'll head back."

Greg pulled me back down. "Come on, stay a while! I'm visiting you!"

"Greg," Officer Lenny warned in his seldom-used authoritative voice. "No touching."

Greg obediently let me go.

"But a new *National Geographic* came in the mail today," I said.

"Flo, you can read it tonight. Come on."

Honestly, it had been a long week, what with Jonathan, Andrew, and the weird mole I'd discovered on my lower back. I'd had about all I could take. "Can we rain-check?"

"Come on," he whined.

"Florence!" someone called from across the room. I looked up and saw Jonathan waving at me.

Wait. Jonathan?

Yes, Jonathan.

The Open Door Jonathan who couldn't take the heat and ran into the kitchen?

Yes, that Jonathan.

"J-Slice!" Nympho Yvette jumped up, intercepting him. "What are you doing here?"

"I'm here to visit Florence."

Nympho Yvette's eyebrows shot up. "You don't say."

"Yep." He said it so casually, like he was visiting my college dorm and not a state prison.

"You know that guy?" Greg asked.

I didn't answer.

"Well, I'll let ya go, but be sure to tell Roy I said hi." Nympho Yvette winked.

"Will do."

Greg watched as Jonathan crossed toward us. "Flo, who is he?"

I considered telling him the truth, but I wasn't sure what the truth was, so I lied. "He's my cousin."

"Hey," Jonathan said. "I hope I'm not interrupting anything."

"I'm Greg."

"Jonathan, this is Greg, he works as a janitor here. Greg, this is Jonathan, my cousin." I gave Jonathan a wide-eyed stare. BE COOL.

Jonathan didn't skip a beat. "Good to meet you, man."

"I'm not just the janitor," Greg said with poorly masked indignity. "Florence and I are best friends."

"Okay. Would you mind if I catch up with my cousin privately?"

Greg bristled. "Sure, I guess I'll leave you to it."

After Greg left, Jonathan sat down. "What up, coz?"

"Sorry about that—"

He waved his hand. "I get it. You don't want to get in trouble because I was a Seminar volunteer."

Huh, good enough. "What are you doing here?"

He rubbed the back of his neck. "I wanted to apologize for last night. I shouldn't have left. I didn't know how to handle that guy bringing up your trial, so I got awkward and ran for it. Fight or flight, I guess. Either way, it was a dick move, and I'm sorry."

"Don't worry about it. I'm a big girl, I handled it."

"Yeah, but having backup would've been nice."

"Maybe," I agreed. "I just hate that my past came up at all."

"You mean you don't like defending your character in public with strangers?" He smiled, his straight, white teeth glistening. "Weird, but okay."

"Why are you here?" The words slipped out of my mouth before I could stop myself.

"I just told you," he said, confused. "To apologize."

"Yeah, but what is your angle?" I asked impatiently. "Normal guys don't come to prison to talk to girls. Did you exhaust your real-world options? Do you think I'd be more open to entertaining whatever sick fetish you have? You know you can go on Craigslist to have someone pee on your cat or whatever you're into."

He looked bewildered. "No, I like you! Why do you always assume I have a fetish just because I want to get to know you?"

"Because it doesn't make sense. You're too normal. Are you trying to make an ex-girlfriend jealous by getting with someone edgy?"

"No, and I don't think that 'getting with' a prisoner would make anyone jealous."

"Then why are you here?"

"I like you!" He laughed. "Like a normal guy likes a normal girl."

"I'm not normal. Look around you!" I exclaimed quietly, so as not to catch the guards' attention. "Admit it, you were curious about prison. Or maybe you wanted something to use for your graduate thesis."

"My thesis is going to have to do with international healthcare costs per capita, which has absolutely nothing to do with prisons. And as far as being curious, my dad went to prison when I was little. I didn't want to visit him then, and to be honest, I don't like being here now."

"I didn't ask you to come. You could have waited until my Seminar."

"I don't like things hanging over my head, especially when it's my fault."

I eyed him suspiciously. "So you are here because you like me, and you want to get to know me?"

He sighed with relief. "Yes."

"You're not looking to harvest my organs?"

"No."

"People do steal organs."

"I'm not stealing your organs."

"There's probably half a liver being sold on Craigslist as we speak."

"I don't know about your liver, but your lungs suck. I heard you hacking when we had dinner. They wouldn't be worth harvesting."

"I was choking on pancake!" I said. "Besides, my kidneys would go for a good buck on the black market. I'm hydrated as hell."

"Børis and Vladamir vill be gläd to hær it."

I broke into a smile.

"Any more working theories about me?" Jonathan asked.

"Not yet." I hesitated. "Actually, I do have a question. How do you know Yvette?"

Jonathan smiled. "She's always seated in my section during the Seminars. She has a thing for one of the other waiters, and she asks me to relay messages to him."

"And you do?"

"I'm a sucker for shock value," he admitted.

"What does she tell you to say to him?"

Jonathan squinted up the ceiling. "I believe the last thing she said was, 'I want to climb your tree and pick your coconuts.'"

"I don't even know what that means."

"Me neither." He grinned. "But he hates it."

I laughed, but there was still a ball of unease rolling around in my stomach. "I need you to ask me questions."

"What kind of questions?"

"I need you to ask me why I'm here. I know you have questions, and I can't trust you if you don't ask."

"Okay." He nodded. "I do have a few."

"Ask them."

"How long were you and your ex together?"

My heart quickened. I opened this door. I shouldn't have, but I did. I took a breath. "Little over three years."

"Was it a good relationship?"

"I thought it was." Images of Charlie Gibson licking our melting sherbet-twist ice cream cones appeared; I shook my head to dispel the useless memory. "In retrospect, we were too different. I thought that opposites attracted, but you can't fit a square peg in a round hole without doing some damage."

"Who incurred the damage?" he asked.

"Right after the breakup, I would've said me." I took a deep breath and exhaled sharply. "He was a strong personality, and I lost some of myself in that, but according to the psychologist here, whenever a relationship isn't a good fit, it takes a toll on both people."

"How long were you broken up when he was killed?"

"Five months."

"Did you see him a lot between the breakup and his murder?"

"Only once."

"The day he was killed?"

I looked at him quizzically.

Jonathan hesitated. "I read about your trial last night on Wikipedia."

"I'm on Wikipedia," I repeated in disbelief.

"Yes. But it's a short page."

"Does it have my picture on it?"

"Yeah . . ."

"Is it at least a flattering picture?"

"Um . . ."

"Awesome."

We sat in silence for a minute.

"What other questions do you have for me? About the murder, my alibi, any of the juicy stuff? I'm sure Wikipedia didn't cover everything."

"It didn't," he replied. "But I'm more interested in you than your crime."

Heat filled my cheeks.

"Why do you believe I'm innocent? Really?"

"All right." He stretched his legs. "Remember your first Seminar? Your date didn't stop talking the whole time?"

I thought back to that night with Harrison. "Yes."

"There was a point where he got embarrassed by something, and instead of enjoying the silence, you said something that made him feel so much better that he talked nonstop for the rest of the night."

I smiled. "I told him that my dad doesn't believe in the moon landing."

"You were kind, and I figured if you killed someone, it was an accident or self-defense. So when you said you didn't do it, it made sense."

"Okay." I nodded. "I can live with that. But let's have one ground rule."

"What?" he asked.

"No visiting me here ever again. For both our sakes."

He smiled. "Deal."

When I got back from the visitation room, the gritty white walls of my cell practically shimmered with excitement. I leaped onto my bed and flailed like a silent dolphin. It was the only outlet I had for the exorbitant amount of hormonal energy coursing through my veins. My fingertips, among other things, tingled happily, and my chest filled with warmth. I clutched a pillow to my smiling goober face.

"Florence!" I heard Nympho Yvette yell down the block.

"What?" I yelled back into the pillow.

"If you think we aren't going to talk about Jonathan, you are out of your mind."

"What's there to talk about?"

Voices exploded down the block with a creative range of profanities. I grinned to myself; I knew that would get to them. Playing dumb was useless now that Jonathan had shown up in the flesh.

"All right, what do you want to know?"

To my utter lack of surprise, Nympho Yvette started the grilling. "How long has this been going on? Did you know he was coming today? How big is it? I'm talking length by width by girth."

"A few weeks, I didn't know he was coming, and I have no knowledge of his dimensions."

"Who is Jonathan? Where did you meet him?" First Lady Abigail hollered.

I bit my lip. I had to be careful. The first rule of Decaf: Don't talk about Decaf. "He's a friend from college."

Thankfully, no one from Decaf tried to correct me.

"I thought you had a 'no dating ever again' rule," Yosemite Karen yelled back. It's amazing how you don't need to see someone's face to know she is being a snarky twat.

"Unlike middle school, a guy can talk to a girl even if they don't 'like like' each other."

"So you're just friends?"

"Yep."

"Like you and Greg?" Susie the Strangler teased.

"No, Greg and I are platonic friends. Nothing will ever, ever, ever happen between us. Jonathan and I have chemistry."

"So you *are* a couple!" Susie the Strangler exclaimed.

"We aren't going to hook up or date. We're just going to flirt a lot."

"You guys are going to be 'friends with benefits' without the benefits?" Nympho Yvette yelled, repulsed. "What's the point? Might as well sew up your vagina and call it a day!"

"He obviously likes you if he drove out here to visit you," one of the Domestics added.

"He does like me," I said nonchalantly.

"He told you that?!" Nympho Yvette yelled. "Did you say it back?"

"Yeah, he said it, but I didn't say it back. That's the number one rule of Sexy Friendship: you can't tell the other person that you like them back. That way it never advances to a relationship."

"What is a 'Sexy Friendship'?" Lovely Elizabeth asked.

"It's an alternative to relationships that I just came up with. It's governed by a set of rules that I've established based on life experience and common sense. Eventually, I'm going to patent it." I paced my cell, the linoleum floor scraping against my grippy socks. "All the fun with no commitment."

"It's ridiculous how against commitment you Millennials are," Yosemite Karen complained.

"Commitment is a tool of the patriarchy to bridle independent women," Feminist Lorraine said. "For every woman tied down to the railroad of marriage, there is a train of a man barreling toward her to destroy her."

"What's wrong with being with one person for the rest of your life?" Susie the Strangler asked. "I've been with Phil for over three decades, and even though it hasn't all been peaches and cream, I'm grateful I have him."

"There's nothing wrong with that," I called back. "But I will function better in a Sexy Friendship than in a relationship."

The advantage of lifelong monogamy was not lost on me. Many people do monogamy, and do it well: my parents, my grandparents, Kristen Bell and Dax Shepard, Bonnie and Clyde. I believed that monogamy worked, and worked toward the common good, but it was messy for me. I never managed to do it well.

"You think that Jonathan will be into a Sexy Friendship?" Nympho Yvette called. "AKA Castration?"

"He'll love it."

"And if he doesn't?"

"Then he can be on his way."

"He seems like a caring soul," Lovely Elizabeth said. "Be careful not to mistreat him. I witnessed him speaking with you, and he has love in his eyes."

"He wants to slip it to Florence long-term," Nympho Yvette agreed.

"How would I mistreat him?"

"Just don't lead him on."

"Or be really, really mean and cynical like you normally are," Yosemite Karen said bluntly. "Give him a fighting chance."

"Why are you rooting for him at all? When Yvette told you about Francesco, you insisted that he was a serial killer!"

"Maybe I want you to get murdered," she yelled.

Susie the Strangler stepped in. "We're just telling you to let your guard down and see where things go. Jonathan's not your ex, he doesn't know your ex, and you can't assume that he's going to do what your ex did."

"Oh, you mean get himself killed?"

"See! That! That is bitchy," Yosemite Karen said. "Susie is trying to give you genuinely good advice, and you're doing your defensive bitchy thing. Just don't do that with the new guy, and you might actually enjoy your Sexy Friendship."

Despite the implication that I was an emotionless shrew, they had a point. Maybe it was time to ever-so-slightly lower my guard with Jonathan.

CHAPTER 25

Dat Mexicano

Brisk gusts of autumn air pushed me through The Open Door's entrance like the insistent hand of God saying, "I love you. Now don't be a chicken shit." So between the unbundling and re-bundling, Jonathan and I began sharing our lives, one tidbit at a time.

In theory, the task of getting to know someone is preposterously tedious. It's a long psychosexual interview that is tricky for three reasons:

1. You have to be yourself, but not the full-on version of yourself that your friends and family know. You can't be bra-lessly fisting Nutella into your mouth when you first meet someone. You've gotta pace yourself. That's the stuff that they'll get to find out when it's too late to back out.

2. You need to figure out who the other person is. They're going to be hiding their unattractive qualities too. They're not going to tell you that they secretly smoke, are constantly late, and stare at their boogers when they blow their nose. You have to try to wade through the bill-paying, omelet-mak-

ing version they're peddling and find out who they actually are.

3. You have to ignore the hormones pulsing in your ears and figure out what the other person is saying. In the past, I had been on dates where I only caught every other word because all I wanted to do was sit on the guy's face.

It's complicated.

In theory.

In reality, when the person you want to get to know has big blue eyes and a smile so damn beautiful that you want to punch a koala, it's simple.

For me, the best part of getting to know someone is the weird stuff that comes out once you cover the fundamentals. It's great that your favorite color is green, and that you like Taylor Swift, but get to the juicy stuff. Tell me that you only have seven toes because a falcon swooped down and mauled you. Tell me that you wear a foil hat when the Celtics play because it's good luck. Tell me your grandfather is Poseidon. Tell me something good.

"You're Mexican?" I asked incredulously. My date's Crohn's disease had driven him to the bathroom for the third time that night, giving Jonathan and me a chance to actually have a conversation during a Seminar.

"*Si, soy mexicano,*" he responded, stroking an invisible mustache, white makeup smudging underneath his fingertips. It appeared that The Open Door took Halloween rather seriously, and for the entire month of October, the staff was mandated to wear costumes. Jonathan was currently Dracula, which was fun, but nothing compared to his tooth fairy costume. Man thighs never looked so dignified.

"Do you think you're the first white kid to try and convince me that he's only half-vanilla? No, good sir, you're not. You are vanilla bean at most. Certainly not fried ice cream."

"You don't believe me?" He smiled with his eyes.

"Look at you." I scrutinized him. "I am tanner than you are."

"That doesn't mean I'm not Mexican."

"Okay, maybe enough to get a scholarship."

"*Oh, but señiorita,* I am fifty percent Mexican!"

"Come on. Like Mexican Mexican?"

"Sí!"

"Like your-family-plays-in-a-Mariachi-band Mexican?"

"Florence!" he blurted out, laughing. "My last name is Diaz!"

Bekah walked past us with a tray of hot comfort food. Brown, fried chicken legs floated in rivers of gravy on mounds of mashed potatoes.

"Bekah!" I whisper-yelled.

"Hold on." She unloaded the tray for a table of overweight office receptionists who licked their lips as steam lifted off the chicken. They sipped their Diet Pepsis in unison and dove in.

Bekah came back to our table, wiping her hands on her pants. "What's up?"

"Is Jonathan Mexican? Look at me. Don't look at him." I put my hand over Jonathan's eyes.

"Yeah." She laughed, straightening the tail on her T-Rex costume. "He's Mexican. I don't know how. He's stupid white even without the Dracula makeup on. He's like Albino Mexican." She grabbed a water pitcher off the table next to us and left to refill glasses.

"Wow." I turned to Jonathan. "Then what I said was slightly offensive."

He patted my arm. "You're a huge racist."

I rolled my eyes.

He grinned back, his azure eyes beckoning me to picnic under an apple tree and fall asleep in the dappled sunlight slipping through the autumn leaves. I hated to be a mushy sap, but that sapphire gaze made me want to dry hump under the Northern Lights.

CHAPTER 26

Charisma

Entertainment was scarce in prison, so unsurprisingly, the other inmates were eating up my Sexy Friendship like tiramisu. They wanted the nitty-gritty details: what he said, how he said it, and how he smelled when he said it. They wanted to know it ALL.

It was a bizarre experience. When I started dating my ex, no one liked him, so no one ever asked about him. I could see why now. He was an accountant who laughed at people who were bad at Excel, a philosopher who avoided meeting my friends, and an agnostic who had no time for meaningful belief. To say that my family and friends tolerated him would be an overstatement, and to say that they hated him is too disparagingly accurate. Nonetheless, they pasted on smiles and begrudgingly spent holidays and birthdays with him.

Of course, no one tells you how they feel about your boyfriend until after you break up. Then they come out of the woodwork with lists, often written, of what they hated about him. Even my mother, the anti-hater, told me about all the reasons my ex and I were wrong for each other from the start.

But weirdly enough, the inmates who knew Jonathan *liked* him, and the ones who didn't liked what they heard.

Nympho Yvette squealed with delight as we ruminated over his physique (which *clears throat unconvincingly* I would NEVER do because that would be objectifying him), Susie the Strangler demanded a play-by-play of every moment, and even Feminist Lorraine had grown to like Jonathan tales ever since I told her that his grandmother was a little-known suffragette who had been imprisoned for her radical political stand.

It wasn't true, of course. For all I knew, Jonathan's grandmother was a white supremacist who gleefully submitted to her husband's will, but the lie made Feminist Lorraine so happy. I couldn't break it to her.

"Was she one of the ten that picketed Woodrow Wilson in 1917?" she asked, putting anti-frizz gel in Becky Bear's hair.

Cosmetology/Astrology Therapy, like every other group therapy, was held in the positive interaction rooms, but our "therapist" Gwen made the place unrecognizable by filling the walls with posters of constellations, French braids, supernovas, and extravagant up-dos. On the blackboard, she drew the planets and mapped their trajectories amidst hand-drawn bobby pins and combs.

"His grandmother was a relatively unheard-of activist," I lied. "She did some local stuff in . . . wherever Jonathan's family was from."

"Ah!" Feminist Lorraine sighed. "What I would give to be one of those pioneering women! The bravery it took to speak out when no one was listening!"

"No one is still listening," Greg said, peeking his head into the room.

"Get out of here," Nympho Yvette yelled playfully. "Girl time!"

"Go on, get!" Susie the Strangler said in her most hick-ish tone.

Gwen, the green-tea-drinking Bohemian who read the stars and taught us how to fishtail braid, sauntered over. "You can stay, Gregory. The cosmos told me you needed to be here today." She bowed and walked back to brush out Gretchen's rat-nest hair.

"Anyways," Feminist Lorraine resumed, "can you ask Jonathan if he has any newspaper clippings of the rallies she was in? I would love to take a look."

"Jonathan, your cousin?" Greg asked.

Oh crap.

"Cousin? No, Flo's new Sexy Friend." Nympho Yvette twirled Caroline/Carolyn/Coraline's hair into a bun. "How do you not know that?"

"Good question," he said slowly. "Why haven't I heard about it? And why did you say that he was your cousin?"

Fine, so I hadn't gone out of my way to inform Greg about my Sexy Friendship. Maybe I didn't want to rub it in his face. Or maybe I was a totally avoidant wimp.

"We've been getting to know each other, and I lied about him being my cousin because it's not a relationship and I didn't want anyone jumping to conclusions."

"Where the hell did you meet him?" Greg picked up a scrunchie and stretched it in his hands. "The only time you meet—"

"Yeahhhh," I said guiltily.

His face distorted with disgust. "YOU MET HIM AT—"

"COLLEGE," Lovely Elizabeth interrupted with big, terrified eyes.

"What?"

"Yes!" I jumped in. "I met him in *college,* Greg. We took a class together on confidentiality and *the horrible things that happen when a person talks about things they shouldn't.*"

Greg looked at Gwen, the guards, and all the non-Decafers. He seemed to get the hint. "Well, I can't believe you met this guy at *college*, and now all of a sudden, he's your boyfriend!"

"He's not my boyfriend," I moaned. "This is why I didn't tell you. I knew you'd jump to conclusions."

"So he's not your boyfriend?" Greg asked.

"No."

"Do you like him?"

"I don't know." I shrugged.

"What is he like?"

"Um . . . he's likable . . . kind of charismatic."

I didn't know if that was a good description, but it was the only thing I could think of quickly. Was charismatic a church denomination? Did I just describe Jonathan as a deacon of a snake church? I didn't know. Maybe Greg wouldn't either, and he would drop it.

"I don't trust charisma."

Susie the Strangler leapt like she'd be pinched. "What do you mean you don't trust charisma?!"

Gwen sprayed detangler in Gretchen's hair. "Greg, being charismatic means being charming and likeable."

"I know what it means," Greg snapped. "It's a dishonest quality."

"What's dishonest about it?" Lovely Elizabeth asked.

"Charismatic people are trying to hide something. He probably has a gambling addiction or a couple of wives stashed in his basement. Don't trust him, Flo. He's for sure trying to cover something up."

Susie the Strangler crossed her arms. "I think you are peeved about Florence meetin' someone."

"No! I just got a bad feeling about the guy!"

"I suppose I will figure it out as time goes on," I cooed maternally.

"Well, I gotta go," he muttered. "See ya." The keys on his waistband jingled as he skulked away.

Seeing Greg upset was disheartening, but it was inevitable. Plenty of other cons could make him happy! His perfect woman was probably jumping rope with her ex's intestines as we spoke. I knew his true love would find him someday, but she needed to get convicted first.

True love waits.

CHAPTER 27

The Trifecta

Greg's demeanor continued to wilt as Thanksgiving approached. Normally, he'd sneak me a pumpkin spice latte every few days, but I had been left pumpkinless all season long. Where was I? GUANTANOMO BAY??[21]

Instead, Greg took to slowly lurking past my cell like a sad puppy with scoliosis. Every day, he made sure I saw his gloomy display before he moved on. If it weren't such an obvious ploy for pity, I might have felt bad. But I didn't. If anyone should've felt bad, it should've been him.

Because while he was playing the victim, he missed out on the trifecta of horrific November dates.

First there was Two Bear. You know the type: if you have one bear, he has two bears. If you haven't encountered a Two Bear, then you yourself may be a Two Bear. Are you a one-upper? Do you have an arsenal of kickass stories that you use to make people feel terrible? Are you in constant competition with people without their knowledge? If so, then you are a Two Bear. When I told Two Bear that I had a turtle as a kid, he told me that he saved an endangered leather-backed turtle from poachers in Tanzania. When I mentioned that my dad had ac-

---

21 Yeah, I hear myself.

cidentally forgotten my sixteenth birthday, he disclosed that his abusive father told him that he was adopted on his deathbed. No matter what story I had, Two Bear crushed it with his tales of devastation and glory. You can never win against a Two Bear. Remember that.

Then there was Alcoholic Frat Boy—my favorite of the Seminar wildlife. He told me that I was "hot, like really hot. Not in that MILF way, but, like . . . in a really hot way," and then he barfed all over me. It smelled like hot wings and seeped, warm and chunky, into each gap of my button-up shirt. Jonathan ran to my rescue with pathetic helplessness in his eyes and tried to clean up the mess. As embarrassing as it was, him wiping partially digested bar food off of me was the most action I'd gotten in years. Bless his soul.

Lastly, there was The Troubadour, who was doing some hard-hitting musical research for his next album. His mom's basement wasn't offering him any inspiration, so he decided to encounter the darkest character he could: me. The temptation to lie about the dozens of murders I had gotten away with was outweighed by the looming evaluation he would have to fill out at the end of the Seminar. The last thing I needed was to get convicted of other murders I didn't commit. So, I didn't mess with The Troubadour, and he was so touched by my openness that, at the end of dinner, he decided to share a song with me. He pulled out his guitar, hummed, and began, "TO-DAY IS GUNNA BE THE DAY THAT THEY'RE GUNNA THROW IT BACK TO YOU!!!"

Fuck. That. Wonderwall. Song.

Despite the horrors of Decaf, November was still the best time of year to be incarcerated at Coffee. Thanksgiving food drives hooked us up with every type of gravy, stuffing, and cranberry sauce known to man. The apple cider was plentiful, and this year, we indulged in a turducken—the supernal melding of all voluptuous bird meats. As a foodie (fat kid trapped in a size 8 body), I reveled in being able to test the spandex waist of my jumpsuit.

My mother sat patiently in the visitation room wearing her turkey sweatshirt with the ironed lace collar. She smiled sadly. Holidays were hard for her. She missed me, and despite my attempts to downplay it, I missed her too.

"I'm sorry your dad isn't here." She placed her warm hand on mine. "He's volunteering at Salvation Army with the bowling league."

"Tell him I love him," I said, giving her a hug. "Happy early Turkey Day. Gobble, gobble."

"You too, honey. Gobble, gobble."

She looked tired. I wondered what toll my life had taken on her. On days like today, I feared she'd lost years. The areas of her face reserved for stress and sorrow seemed overworked, and lines had etched deep into her soft skin. No amount of apologizing would ever be sufficient, so all I could do was listen intently as she shared the recipes she was cooking this year and told me which ones she was planning to make next year when I would be joining them.

"Maybe Greg could come over next year." She grinned like this was the first time the thought ever occurred to her. "Maybe he'd appreciate my pine nut stuffing."

"Nut stuffing." I snickered.

"Why?" she asked, exasperated.

I shrugged.

"Invite Greg."

"He's not too happy with me right now," I replied, "and I doubt it'll pass in a year; that boy can hold a grudge."

"What did you do?"

"Wow, why do you assume I did something?"

"If you didn't do anything, then what happened?"

I hadn't decided whether or not I was going to tell my mom about Jonathan. She was a diehard Greg fan, plus I wasn't sure how to explain my Sexy Friendship without her hearing wedding bells. A casual relationship would be foreign to a woman like my mother, who grew up with terms like "courting" and "going steady." She wanted a son-in-law (and half a dozen grandkids), not an uncommitted Sexy-Friend-in-law.

"Greg has got some personal stuff going on," I said, glossing over the finer points.

"Oh, I was afraid you two had a falling out." She smiled. "He is a really nice boy, and *you never know.*"

CHAPTER 28

Moody with a Side of Meatballs

You know when you're so hungry that you could repeatedly stab someone in the face?

Well, Crazy Jessie got that hungry.

On Black Friday, the kitchen ran out of mac 'n' cheese, and she lost it. She screamed, "GIVE ME THE G-DAMN CHEESIEST!" and stabbed one of the chefs in the eye with a soupspoon. It was gruesome. A fountain of blood and sclera ran out of the chef's eye socket like an over-easy egg at the Red Wedding. As far as stabbings went, Crazy Jessie could've done worse. That particular chef was lax with her hairnet use and constantly shed into our food. Nonetheless, they put Crazy Jessie in a straightjacket and hauled her off to a spoon-less rubber room in a mental institution far, far away.

(A moment of silence for a fallen crazy comrade.)

The stabbing wasn't even the worst part—okay, well, it was, but the aftermath was a close second: the entire kitchen staff was mandated to attend eighty hours of off-site trauma therapy to assess for psychological damage. That meant that for the first two weeks of December, all we ate was stale bread and canned vegetables. To make matters worse, in that fortnight, PMS hit like a motherfucking heavyweight champ. You want to know the trick to keeping a bunch of iron-deficient, emotional female prisoners happy? Chocolate. But no chefs meant no chocolate. No chocolate cakes, no chocolate pies, no chocolate cookies, not even a chocolate chip pancake! Idiots! They were all idiots! Why didn't they have a backup chocolate plan? You should always have a backup chocolate plan![22]

Not to mention that Greg, in his infinite wisdom, chose the middle of that week to start talking to me again. Most people can read a room, but not Greg. No, he decided to dive into the shallow end, head first.

He sauntered over at lunch. "If you want to have a 'Sexy Friendship,' that's okay. For the record, I think there's something off about the guy, and you could do better, but obviously, you are you, so you aren't going to listen to me. I'll still be here while you learn the hard way."

"I don't get paid to babysit, so go act like a child somewhere else."

"I wasn't—"

"And for the record, I don't need your permission to talk to another guy. I'm not your girlfriend, so if I wanted to bang Charles Manson, it would be none of your business."

"You know what?" Greg burst out. "Don't say I didn't warn you! You deserve whatever happens to you!"

---

22 Sure, us Decafers could get chocolate once a week at our Seminars, but only one meal once a week? That wasn't enough to get my chocolate tank off "empty."

"Apparently, we aren't the only ones PMSing!"

"YOU ARE BEING SUCH—"

"Gregory!" The Warden emerged from the kitchen, sweat dripping down his curled lip. Greg's face went powdered-donut white. "The kitchen floors are filthy, but here you are wasting time by clucking at prisoners like it's a damn roost! I could have hired immigrants to fill your position, but no, I thought, 'Give the kid a chance.'"

"Sir—"

"Why do I bother keeping you here? Have you been a failure since you came out of your failure mother's cunt, or was it something you learned along the way? If you ask me, you are the product of fucking generational sin, and you'd do well cut off your pecker and end the curse."

Holy cow, he used the C word! Feminist Lorraine said only women could use that!

Greg lifted his head. "If anyone is handing down generational sin, it's you. When are you cutting off your Johnson?"

The Warden's face looked like it was about to explode. "Get back to work, you overpaid sack of shit."

Whatever chutzpah Greg had mustered left him, and he scurried into the kitchen to clean something.

The Warden's fat baby face flushed red like a strawberry. "Lenny, take this one to Dr. Sean's office."

Officer Lenny handcuffed me gently. "Let's go, Peach."

I walked silently until the Warden was out of earshot. "I didn't do anything wrong!"

"I know. Seems to me that Greg's feelin' a little threatened by the new guy and lost his head."

I eyed Officer Lenny. "How—"

"I'm a bit of an eavesdropper." He smiled widely, multiplying his wrinkles. "Don't fret. Your secret's safe with me." He opened Dr. Sean's door and unlocked my handcuffs. "Good luck."

Dr. Sean was cleaning his wire glasses on his maroon sweater vest, and he looked up with half-blind eyes. "Take a seat, Florence."

I lowered myself into the worn-out armchair across from him. "Before we start, it's not my fault that Greg flipped out. He blew up over nothing."

Dr. Sean scratched his furrowed brow with his thumb. "I'm debriefing everyone on Jessica stabbing Chef Geraldine. What's going on with Greg?"

"Oh," I said. "Nothing. He just yelled at me—no big deal."

"What was he yelling about?"

I hesitated. "I can't say."

"Everything you say is kept confidential, and unless you are going to hurt yourself or others, I can't disclose it to anyone."

"It's nothing like that. Greg and I are, as you would put it, 'experiencing relational tension'"—I put the phrase in air quotes—"due to him having feelings for me, and me not feeling the same way."

"He told you this?"

My stomach dropped. "I don't want to get him in trouble."

"It's confidential." He shook his head quickly. "Greg said that he has feelings for you?"

Apparently, Dr. Sean was a secret gossip girl. That was okay; he couldn't be above every vice.

"He's never said it out loud, but it's common knowledge. All the inmates and guards know about it, at least. Surprised that they didn't tell you. Aren't the guards supposed to be your eyes and ears?"

"More or less," he admitted, "but they've never reported Greg being inappropriate."

"They wouldn't have." I shrugged. "He's not sexually inappropriate—he only hints that we should date."

"Which you are against?"

"In every way, shape, and form. I've tried to let him down gently in the past, but he didn't get the hint."

"What made him get the hint today?"

I wasn't going to tell Dr. Sean about Jonathan. Sexy Friendships and psychologists don't mix. I didn't need him digging into my psyche trying to understand my genius patent-pending relationship solution. So I glossed over some details.

"Let's just say I made it clear that nothing was going to happen between us, and he didn't take it well. It's fine. Soon I won't be around, and he'll be fine. In the meantime, things will be awkward, but that's life."

"Isn't it though?" Dr. Sean leaned back in his chair, staring out into space. "Do me a favor, tell me if Greg crosses a line. I need to know if he's causing trouble for you or any other prisoner." He shook his head. "It seems you are the only person here who will tell me what's going on."

"I didn't mean to shake your faith in your guard cronies," I said. "I'm sure they tattle about most things."

"Probably, but please tell me if something happens."

"Okay." I shrugged again. "I doubt there'll be much more to report."

"Hopefully not." He scanned the framed degrees on his wall. "I give you credit for addressing the situation with Greg. It's difficult to confront people when you know the truth will upset them."

My temper flared with my nostrils. "That's ironic coming from you."

Dr. Sean's eyebrows rose up his prematurely balding head. "Why's that?"

"Never mind. I'm not trying to be combative."

"This is a safe place, Florence. If you have something to say, say it."

The prospect of this conversation had kept me up nights. I had imagined the argument fifty different ways, and it always ended with Dr. Sean's tail between his legs.

I measured every word carefully. "You repeatedly told me that you were recommending my release, but then I ended up serving the whole five-year term. You thought lying was kinder than the truth, but for future reference, it would've been easier to stomach if you had been upfront with me." I bit my pinky nail down to regulation size. "We both know it's because I won't admit to the murder."

"You made it clear that you would never confess to that, and I made it clear that we'd work around it," he said calmly. "I never doubted your progress, but there were other factors beyond my control, trust me."

"Like what?" I asked.

He opened his mouth, shut it, and opened it again like a hungry, hungry hippo. He shook his head. "It's best to look forward and continue doing what you're doing. Focusing on the past can be toxic."

Coward.

"Debrief me on Jessie, and let me go back to my cell."

CHAPTER 29

Winter Nights

Heavy snowflakes piled on the windowsill outside my cell, while the smooth green plane beneath caught the starry freckles from above. I imagined the sleeping koi fish lining the bottom of the pond like giant bright orange sardines. With the chemical plant nearby closed for the night, the air was almost palatable again. All was quiet.

Silence often tiptoed the line between being redemptive and dangerous. It was sweet relief when you were no longer forced to listen to therapists or guards or prisoners—the darkness of night giving you the space to breathe and think and be for the first time all day. But therein lay the danger. The space could be filled with flowers or demons, and you never knew which until the sun set.

It had been a while since there'd been flowers.

She filled most of the space. I had never formally met her, a fact for which I used to be grateful, but now it was a curse. Every good quality I could fathom was laid upon Her head. In my mind, She was patient and assertive, stable and spontaneous, funny and brilliant. I imagined Her at the post office, at animal shelters, and at parties. I imagined Her conversations, the sound of Her voice, and how She might use Her hands when She spoke.

I envisioned Her with him— the life they would've shared if he hadn't been killed. I imagined them at their dinner table, in the park, and running 5k's. I imagined their children, with handsome eyes and silky hair, running through a sprinkler.

It didn't matter if my eyes were opened or closed; She was there, waiting. So I stared at the dense snowfall, hoping the cold would freeze my mind like the sage pond below.

The next morning, I awoke to the sight of my own breath suspended above my face. According to the guards, Old Faithful had died around 2 a.m. The affectionately named furnace had been around since the war (it was unclear exactly which war) and had lived a long and heated life. Thick orange extension cords wove through the cell block like tree roots, powering small, individual space heaters. Our teeth tap-danced against each other as we waited for the measly towers to heat up our frigid cells.

"It's so cold in here. I'm sure you ladies could cut glass," Officer Carmel commented as he strolled down the hall. "Unzip, Lorraine. Show me those frozen itty bitty titties."

"Eat shit."

He ignored her. "How about you, Yvette? You're always bragging about how sexy you are. Let's see what you got."

"That'd be throwing pearls to pigs, Carmel. If you want to see a naked woman, go online like everyone else."

"I'll give you a peek," First Lady Abigail said from down the row. I was surprised; Susie might have been right. Maybe First Lady Abigail was going through some pent-up sexual struggle.

By the grunts of approval, Carmel was impressed with her cold, pointy nipples. "Merry early Christmas to me," he groaned.

Merry early Christmas to us all.

Unlike Thanksgiving, Christmastime at Coffee sucked mistletoe. Each year, it felt like Santa's reindeers were sitting on our chests, slowly suffocating us.

The little TVs mounted in the corners of our cells mocked us with happy sweater-wearing families and heartwarming Christmas specials. It was hard to watch when everyone we cared about was a barbed wire fence and at least fifty miles away. Of course, we had each other, but we weren't family. We weren't sitting by a toasty fire reminiscing about Uncle Ted's funny egg-nog disaster; we were rats, trapped in our cold cages with mini undecorated Christmas trees slumped next to our toilets. But mostly, we were lonely.

In retrospect, it was a blessing that I didn't have nostalgic holiday memories with my ex. I could remember him pushing his fine brown hair out of his fine brown eyes and lecturing me about consumerism/Christmas's pagan roots/deteriorating church traditions/blah, blah, blah. He was a huge Christmas bummer who fought tooth and nail against the sham of Christmas, and sadly, because relationships make people weak-willed lemmings, I went along with it.

I pretended to respect his gutsy countercultural take on the holidays, but deep down it killed me, because I was a junkie. My drug of choice: Christmas spirit, uncut. I loved the weather, the smells, the church services, the caroling: the whole kit and caboodle. My mother often theorized that her real daughter had been switched at birth with a Christmas elf. How I ever fell for the Grinch was beyond me. Opposites attract, right?[23] Thankfully, my Sexy Friendship was sure to offer a more enlightened perspective on the holidays.

"My family is Jewish," Jonathan said.

NOOOOOO. WHY WAS I ONLY ATTRACTED TO MEN WITH A CHRISTMAS ALLERGY? FIRST SCROOGE, NOW HOTTIE HANUKKAH!

"You don't celebrate at all? What about eggnog or ugly sweater parties?" I asked hopefully.

"The only tradition my family has is burning Christmas trees and knocking down the neighbors' icicle lights. We call it our 'War on Christmas.'" He smiled, apparently fondly remembering the cries of the neighborhood children.

I stared, horrified.

"Kidding." He laughed. "I don't think that Mexican Jews actually exist."

"Oh, thank goodness."

"I've never had eggnog though."

---

23 JK, that's something people say to convince themselves that the reason they are unhappy is because of a personality clash, and not because their significant other is a douche (or doucheé).

"Never?"

"At this point, I'm avoiding it on principle because it sounds gross. What are egg nogs? Or do you nog the egg? If so, what is nogging?"

"Who cares? It tastes like a melted vanilla milkshake! Add a little rum, and"—I kissed the tips of my fingers and flung the kiss to the heavens—"you have to try it."

"I'll make you a deal." He considered me for a moment. "If you make it from scratch—pour your blood, sweat, and tears into it—I will try it."

"Perfect! I've made some in my toilet, so I'll bring it in. In honor of your Mexican Hanukkah."

"*Oy gracias.*" He smiled, then bit his lip. "Actually, I did get something for you. For regular Christmas."

My first instinct was to flip the table and run.

I had hoped against hope that he wouldn't get me anything for Christmas. Gift-giving is a science, and no one I'd ever dated had mastered the skill. There was always an imbalance of power, resulting in one of the following scenarios:

1. You hate the gift, but you have to fake liking it. *Oh my gosh, a plastic plant, thank you!*

2. You like it, but it's too intense for that stage of the relationship, which either buys him a guilt-induced ticket to second base or, in most cases, a ticket to a singles cruise in March.

3. You read into the gift because you really like him.
   He got me an ice cube tray . . . digesting iced drinks
   burns more calories than digesting hot drinks. Is he
   giving this to me because he thinks I'm fat? Maybe he
   just thinks warm water is gross. Yeah, no, he thinks
   I'm fat.

Keep your gift, dude, I obviously cannot handle your business.

He handed me a small box of chocolate-covered strawberries. Thank goodness, he found the loophole! All food-related gifts (with the exception of ice sculptures, candy accompanied by stuffed animals, and heart-shaped edibles) are acceptable.

"I figured you could eat these before you leave. That way you don't have to smuggle anything out of here."

"That is the most depressingly considerate thing anyone's ever said. Have you done this before?"

"Accommodate the needs of a lovely prisoner such as yourself? Can't say I have, but it is fun. It's like interacting with a secret agent. I have to find incognito ways to talk to you and give you stuff."

"That's an exceedingly positive way to view my predicament." And that's how you know you've found the right Sexy Friend.

CHAPTER 30

New Year's Day

Officer Ramirez rolled out a fat silver television with a cracked corner in front of our beanbag chairs. The screen crackled on.

It was New Year's Day, and we were sequestered in a positive interaction room for Cinema Therapy: a once-a-year event where the guards slept off their hangovers and we were allowed a movie marathon. And every year, the marathon began with the same ironic crowd pleaser: *Clue.*

Despite seeing it four times, I could never remember which ending was the real one. Personally, I thought Colonel Mustard was the obvious choice. He was intimidating, military-trained, and mustachioed. You think scatterbrained Professor Plum could execute a well-orchestrated murder? Come on. And how on earth would Miss Scarlet quickly and quietly flee a crime scene in high heels? Girlfriend would break a toe.

Colonel Mustard was definitely the killer, and my working theory was that he murdered my ex. Because, after mentally cataloging every possible suspect, Colonel Mustard seemed like the most plausible answer.

My ex didn't live life on the edge. He was an accountant in a small firm who frequented Applebee's and never went out on the weekends. He hadn't done drugs since high school, and he was always really generous with his hookers. (Joke. He never solicited a prostitute. And if he did, he wouldn't have been generous; he was a notoriously bad tipper.) It appeared I was the only person who had a problem with him.

Aaaand I was the last one to see him alive. WOMP, WOMP.

I know I shouldn't have talked him after we split, but when there is calling, e-mailing, texting, Facebook-ing, Tweeting, Instagram-ing, and Tumblr-ing, it's hard to make a clean break.

So when, a few months after the breakup, he texted me asking if we could get together, I agreed. He asked to meet at a coffee shop, but I asked him to come to Holly's. She was in Pennsylvania with her family, and I read somewhere that if you talk on your "home turf," you feel more in control. It was a dumb move in retrospect, but I thought getting-back-together sex might be involved, and I didn't want to do it in his Prius.

When he knocked on the door, I answered it sporting a new sundress with sexy lace underwear beneath. I was ready for an apology and some mouth kisses.

After exchanging awkward "how are you"s and "you look good"s, we finally began to talk. He apologized that he disappeared, leaving only The Letter in his wake. He said he was sorry that he didn't discuss what was going on with him. He told me I was one of the most intelligent and kindest women that he had ever known, and I deserved better than that, which was why he owed it to me to tell me that he was going to marry Her.

He paused, waiting for my reaction. I think he wanted my blessing.

HAHAHAHAHAHAHA. My heart was officially and irreversibly pureed.

All I could think was, *WOW. It must be great being the kind of woman who is so captivating that he couldn't go another day without being married to Her. It must be fabulous, really freaking awesome. I hope he eats what She cooks, and actually goes to Her cousin's wedding. Oh, and I hope She loves Game of Thrones and has two vaginas! Wouldn't that be the best?*

He waited for me to thank him for the heads up, and I did thank him. I thanked him for breaking up with me, and for not letting me waste my time on an uncommitted, impulsive jerk like him. I told him that I hoped their marriage was short and miserable, and that when they had kids, both of her vaginas would blow out into one huge cavern that his small penis could never navigate. I then opened the door, watched him go to his car, and waved goodbye with both middle fingers.

Okay, so, it wasn't The High Road. And, FINE, it wasn't even The Middle Road, but it was not The Murder Road. Someone else took that detour, and despite what Holly's nosey neighbor insinuated in open court, I was too busy crying and prying my sexy underwear out of my b-crack to follow him home and murder him.

So my theory: Colonel Mustard with My Scarf in My Ex's Kitchen.

After *Clue* ended, the room reverberated with the snores of guards and inmates alike. Aside from myself, the only two awake were Officer Carmel and First Lady Abigail, who were sitting next to each other on the couch under the same blanket. I didn't even try to do a hand check; ignorance was bliss.

My eyelids were heavy, so I wiggled down in my beanbag chair, the beans hissing at my butt in protest. I drifted off slowly, and gravity gradually took its hold on me. I woke with a start when the dirty tile floor touched my face.

I looked up to see Greg, with his foot on my beanbag chair, smiling at me. "You drool when you sleep."

"You're talking to me again?"

He sighed, lowering himself to my level. "Scooch over."

I steamrolled back onto the chair, and he plopped down. The wave of beans lifted me above him.

"I have an idea." He stared at the ground, his right leg jittering nervously. "We don't talk about Jason."

"Jonathan."

"Yeah."

"Okay, works for me."

"Are you still 'not-dating' him?"

"Yes," I said. "Is this your way of not talking about him?"

"That was the last question," he said. "Sorry I was weird about it. I was stupid. Consider it a mix of being protective and just being a dumb dude. But you're smart, and you can make your own decisions."

"Wow, that's very progressive of you. Normally you'd be all, 'you're falling victim to his charms, you helpless damsel.' Why the change?"

"I've been hanging out with Femi-Nazi Lorraine."

"You know that's not what I call her. It's Feminist Lorraine."

"Tomato, to-mah-to. Seriously though, if I've learned anything in our friendship, it's that you don't take dumb risks. You got a good head on your shoulders."

I smiled. He wasn't perfect, but he was sincere. "Thanks, Greg."

"One more thing, and I promise to never ever bring it up again."

"Okay."

"Promise me that if you decide to start dating him, you tell me. Consider it giving my dumb guy brain time to process things."

"I'm not going to date him."

"But if you do, just let me know?"

"Fine. If I'm struck by lightning, and the electricity courses through my body, altering the very core of my being, resulting in my losing all common sense and deciding to date him, I will tell you."

"Promise?" He extended his pinky.

I was in my late twenties; I wasn't going to be making pinky promises about boys. I looked Greg in the eyes. "I promise."

"Okay." He lowered his pinky finger and smirked. "Then I'm officially talking to you again."

"Lucky me." I grinned, rolling my eyes. Inwardly, I was relieved that Greg was dropping the rock. I didn't like being at odds with my friends, even if they were being selfish butt-knuckles.

Finally, things could go back to normal.

CHAPTER 31

Cutthroat Competition

As winter progressed, my Decaf Seminars became mundane. The crazies must've been hibernating. Most of my dates were regular, lonesome guys who wanted a free meal and somebody to talk to. I couldn't judge them; being lonely, hungry, and bored is the human condition.

Unfortunately, normal Seminars meant no shady phone calls or gastrointestinal emergencies to pull my dates away from the table, which meant I couldn't talk to Jonathan. He was rarely our waiter, and even when he was, my dates were great at maintaining eye contact. I was more than a little agitated by this, but where I found frustration, Jonathan found an exciting opportunity to communicate covertly with me.

He began small: refilling our salt and pepper shakers, volunteering to hang up our coats, and haphazardly bumping into my chair. The impish grin he flashed every time we locked eyes was enough to lure me in. So one day, when Jonathan was clearing the remnants of the neighboring table, I spilled my water and it splashed his ankles. When he looked up to see where the deluge came from, I asked for napkins with a wink. He smiled so wide I thought his face would cramp.

It didn't take long after that—two weeks max—for our playful communicado to devolve into a heated competition of creativity and obnoxiousness.

One week, he ran up to my table in a panic. "I need your menus now!"

My hypochondriac date screamed hysterically and flung his menu. "Anthrax!"[24]

"No, sir." Jonathan filched our menus. "We have a misprint on the new menus saying that we serve our pita bread with red pepper *human* instead of red pepper *hummus*. The FDA is on our tail, and we are one hot minute from being deemed a cannibalistic hot spot."

"That sounds serious, mister," I said.

"It is, ma'am, but don't you worry your pretty head," he replied valiantly. "Everything will be fine. Before I go though, may I recommend the hummus? No humans were harmed in the making of it."

The next week, I "accidentally" dropped six different forks on the floor in order to have him come over and replace them. I blamed it on neuropathy in my hands, a condition I had researched in preparation for the prank.

When I ordered a chocolate crepe with caramel ice cream for dinner that night, my date asked if that was such a good idea.

"Why?" I asked, confused.

---

24 Okay, fine, *most* of my Decaf dates had been boring and normal.

"Your diabetes. I'm not sure sweets are a good idea; it'll make your neuropathy worse."

Oh, yes. Apparently, my date assumed that my fake neuropathy was induced by diabetes. And you know what happens when you assume . . .

"DIABETES? I have a bone marrow disorder!" I had taken this joke very seriously, and familiarized myself with neuropathy and *all* its pathologies thanks to Nympho Yvette and her nurse's aide knowledge. "Just say it, you think I'm fat! If you didn't want me to get dessert for dinner, you should've just said that! Don't pretend to be concerned about my health conditions."

"No, I—" He stumbled over the words. "I don't think you're f—"

Jonathan approached inquisitively, but before he could say anything, I dramatically threw my arm over my eyes. "I'll have the house salad, NO DRESSING! Because I'M SO FAT!"

"That's preposterous! Who told you that?" He knew how to play along like the best of them.

I pointed to my date and dropped my head in defeat.

"No! No! I don't think you're fat. Look, my grandmother has neuropathy in her feet, and she had to get her toes removed. It was because of diabetes."

"Do I look like your grandmother's toeless feet!" I cried hysterically, but not so hysterically that the officers on duty took notice. I could see them in my peripheral vision, nose-deep in their free meals.

"Please, no!" my date pleaded desperately. "I'm so sorry, get the crepe. You—you're perfect the way you are."

"Thank you." I wiped my dry eyes. "I'll have two crepes."[25]

That day, I assumed that the war was won, that I was the champion of well-thought-out hijinks, and all others were dum-dums in comparison to my genius. Who, I asked myself, could possibly top that?

I got my answer a couple weeks later when my date shook my hand, planted himself into his chair and let one rip. It sounded like an angry T. rex had taken up residence in his trousers.

"Um—" My date lifted his skinny-yet-powerful butt out of the chair.

Jonathan came running up to us. "Sir, I am so incredibly sorry. There was a birthday clown convention here early this morning, and I thought I had gotten all of them." Jonathan pulled a deflated whoopee cushion out from my date's seat. "Miss, can I check your seat?"

I stood up and he checked the chair.

"I think we're clear." Jonathan paused and squinted at me. "Except . . ." All of a sudden, he pulled a quarter out of my ear, mumbled, "Damn birthday clowns," and walked away.

I had met my match.

When prisoners teased me for smiling like a goober, I credited a night of freedom and good food as the cure to cabin fever, but we all knew the truth—it was Jonathan with his

---

25 Lest you feel bad for our friend with the toeless diabetic grandmother, it's worth noting that he had lost a bet, and signing up for Decaf was his punishment. He got off easy.

light, clever, easy-going ways. Being around him felt like a sumo wrestler had finally stood up from my chest and my lungs were slowly reinflating. When I was with him, I wasn't Inmate 4557. I was the girl he confided in and flirted with, his partner in crime—figuratively speaking—and it was exhilarating.

Becoming an ordinary person again was exhilarating.

CHAPTER 32

Scandal on the Coffee Express(o)

HAPPY VALENTINE'S DAY!

Don't like Valentine's Day? TOO BAD! NO ONE CAN ESCAPE IT!

Cross the globe, change your address, burn off your fingerprints! Doesn't matter! The plastic hearts and plush teddy bears will still find you. Valentine's Day will not be defeated!

(Wails into a dozen roses.)

Actually, Valentine's Day wasn't a big deal at Coffee. You'd think being alone—or at least isolated from significant others—would be a trigger, but it seemed the Hallmark holiday had lost significance for most of us. Plus, the chefs gave us little chocolates with our dinners, so we were happy campers.

However, Valentine's Day held a different significance to us prisoners. It marked the beginning of a new era of Coffee Beans! The newcomers tentatively filed through the door, chained together in a line.

Traditional prisons have rolling admission, but not Coffee. Coffee needed to keep its therapy and Rehabilitation Board reviews synchronized, so it only accepted prisoners once a year.

Recruitment Week, as we called it, was a mix of orientation and intimidation. Dr. Sean assessed the new arrivals' "strengths and concerns" while the guards flexed hard, convincing the newbies that Coffee was a hardcore prison, not a summer camp for misfit toys.

The newbies were jaded anyways. Due to the once-a-year acceptance policy, the faces that filed in weren't fresh from the courtroom. Most had sat around in local jails waiting, biding their time for this day.

The youngest recruit was Circuit Samantha, a dewy-skinned girl with thinning yellow hair, whose mouth rested in a serious thin plane. She was perhaps ninety pounds soaking wet, and we heard that she had electrocuted her (male) neighbor with jumper cables. They say poison is a woman's weapon, but what of electricity? It's clean and quick—very considerate of the crime scene clean-up crew.[26]

The oldest arrival was Margret Mayweather. She punched her boyfriend in the gut, and he died like Houdini. Then there was Terrifying Gloria. She had bright white hair, with dark pink rosacea spatter on her cheeks. Officer Carmel said that she hog-tied her ex with a bungee cord, and then buried him alive . . . by hand. Odds were she was going to be in that small percentage of inmates that end up in real prison, because that's some callous Hannibal Lecter nonsense.

---

26 Women: eternally concerned with not burdening others.

The newbies hadn't been here two days before First Lady Abigail got caught having sex with Officer Carmel in the supply closet.

Oh yes, you heard me. They did the dirty.

Welcome to Coffee, newbies.

After her years of stalking the POTUS, First Lady Abigail's postcoital description of Carmel's nether regions sounded like a State of the Union address. She shamelessly broadcast his size, his girth, and the curve of his baton, all while he vehemently denied it. Hilarious. Nympho Yvette offered to let Carmel set the record straight, but his pants stayed buckled, and he continued to hide his tiny, slightly left-veering shameful secret.

None of us had expected the last couple months of sexual tension to actually amount to anything, but when Greg went to get more sponges, he stumbled upon their secret fornication.

"I want to pour bleach in my eyes," Greg whimpered, "but I can't because he had her against the bleach . . . and the squeegees . . . and the mop."

"You saw some T and A; you'll be fine." Nympho Yvette waved a hand dismissively and opened a new box of dryer sheets.

Greg fell backward into the dirty laundry basket. "My brain caught an STD when I saw them, and the infection is going to melt my spinal cord. When I'm paralyzed, all I'm going to see is Carmel and—BLAH!"

"You'll survive." I patted Greg on the head. "Just never open any door ever again, and you'll be fine."

"Abigail's such a slut."

"Oh, Abigail is the slut?" I smiled wryly. "Anything to say about Officer Carmel abusing his power by sleeping with her?"

"He's surrounded by women twenty-four seven. What do you expect?"

"Maybe for him to be professional and self-controlled."

"Oh, come on. Girls are the ones who are supposed to be in control of themselves. They don't have the same urges as men," he said matter-of-factly.

Nympho Yvette guffawed, slamming the washing machine closed. "Have you ever had a girlfriend who wasn't inflatable? Girls are just as horny as guys."

"Well, they shouldn't be! Who's going to buy the cow when you can get the milk for free?"

Oh Greg, you misogynic tool. He was lucky Feminist Lorraine was sick in the infirmary today. "Boys will be boys, then?"

"Basically, Flo. Girls got to keep themselves pure, not going around having . . . you know . . ."

"Sex?" Nympho Yvette offered happily.

"Yeah. All I'm saying is that it's the girl's responsibility to say 'yes' or 'no' because with us, it's always yes. It's science."

"You know what's not science? Carmel and Abigail boinking in your supply closet." I snapped him with the towel I was folding.

"OW!"

"Yo!" Officer Garcia hollered. "If I see that again, you're going to solitary."

Margret Mayweather shuddered beside me.

I rolled my eyes.

Solitary confinement was the boogey monster: folklore designed to scare new prisoners into shutting up and cooperating. It wasn't real. In my five years at Coffee, no one had been locked away in a windowless room, though God knows some days I'd shank a broad to get some alone time.

Officer Garcia glared at my irreverence; clearly it wasn't the fearful reaction he wished to elicit. He pointed irresolutely, unsure what threat would be effective, and added half-heartedly, "Just watch it."

"You tell her, Garcia." Greg grinned, rubbing his right tricep. He pulled up his sleeve and craned his neck to see the healthy pink welt developing. "Look what you did!"

"Sorry, I didn't mean to get you that bad."

"It's okay." He smiled tenderly. "You're still my best friend."

I winced.

Greg had been dropping the phrase "best friend" a lot recently, and the more he said it, the more desperate and clingy it sounded. I thought he was subconsciously tightening his hold on me, terrified that I might walk out of Coffee and never look back.

My knee-jerk reaction to his insecurity was YOU'RE SMOTHERING ME, because I was an insensitive oaf. A better person would have sat down with him and addressed his concerns, but I wasn't a better person, I was just me.

So I came up with my own method of dealing with him: every time he suggested we do something post-release, I agreed to do it. It was an easy solution that seemed to sooth his anxious spirit. Thus far, I had agreed to join a bowling league, watch monster truck shows, raise a baby chick, go on a safari, visit Sea World, climb Mt. Everest, tour hot air balloon festivals, and teach English in Guatemala. There weren't enough hours in a day to do half of those things, but it made him feel better, so what the heck?

Admittedly, it was a bad plan. The gritty truth was that Greg and I wouldn't be spending any time together when I got out. If this surprises you, it shouldn't. Unrequited relationships can't last. No one's feelings die down when they spend exorbitant amounts of time with their crush. In high school, I was head over heels for Mike Harvey. He was quiet and funny and handsome and gay. I didn't know that last part until I was already hooked. We did theater together, so we were always practicing lines, gossiping about drama, and laughing at the divas who thought they were Broadway bound. And even though I knew Mike was strictly off-limits, it felt like I'd spilled warm water in my lap every time he was around. It was torture trying to be chill around him when all I wanted to do was jump his gay bones. It took his family moving out of state for the spell to finally break, and when it broke, I recovered and got on with my life.

That was what Greg needed—to be cut off cold turkey. It was the merciful thing to do.

CHAPTER 33

Snowed In

It was February 20, and Officer Ramsey had just parked at The Open Door when an ugly horn blared through the radio, alerting us to the dangers of the current conditions. The governor announced a state of emergency, mandating that all citizens stay off the roads until further notice. It wasn't a shock; the visibility was dirt poor, and on the way to the restaurant, the unmarked police car had swerved left and right, barely clinging to the road.

My outdoorsy date decided that he and his beard were going to brave the storm and hike home. Stranded with nothing to do, I spent the evening hanging out with Jonathan and Bekah, pouring mounds of marshmallows into our hot chocolates.

"He should be a registered sex offender," Bekah said seriously. "He's a predator; humps all the neighborhood children."

"Every day is hump day for Oscar," Jonathan agreed. "He's a horndog. AKA a horny canine."

Bekah threw her hand over her heart. "True, but he's my canine, horny though he may be!"

"Is he a rescue?" I asked.

"Why?" She laughed. "You think he's promiscuous because he suffered some puppyhood trauma or something?"

"Maybe!"

"Nah, he just has a strong sex drive because we never got him fixed. My dad wanted to breed him, but it ended up that he's a knucklehead and low on the reproduction totem pole. We'd neuter him, but humping gives him so much joy."

"He ruined a pair of my jeans last time I visited," Jonathan told me solemnly.

"You've met Bekah's dog?"

A corner of me had wondered if there was something between Jonathan and Bekah. He didn't seem interested, but she was a harder read.

"Jonathan watched my younger brother Matthew when my family was going out of town. Matthew refused to miss his soccer tournament, which was stupid. He's only in third grade— it's not like his team was going to states."

"They won that weekend. I've never seen the Baby Bears play so hard."

"Did anyone throw up from exertion? No? Well, there you go. Must not have played that hard."

Jonathan rolled his eyes. "Bekah is leaving in a couple weeks to play soccer for the University of Barcelona, so she's become a bit of a soccer snob."

"I prefer fanatic."

My brain was half-frozen on the image of Jonathan taking care of children. My maternal instinct kicked up in my chest. *JONATHAN IS GOOD WITH KIDS.*

Thankfully, my logic jumped in about then. *Heel, girl. You don't even know that he is good with them. He could've kept the kid locked up in the basement while he did exorbitant amounts of heroin. Don't give him too much credit.*

Once my brain thawed, I looked at Bekah. "The University of Barcelona? Are you in college?"

"Yeah, I'm a freshman. How old did you think I was?"

"My age."

"Nope, nineteen in July. I'll be back from Barcelona before then, though. SUMMER VACAY!"

"Jonathan, how old are you?" I hoped my age meter wasn't wonky.

"Sixteen."

Bekah balled up a straw wrapper and threw it at his head. "Don't mess with her. He's twenty-seven. How old are you?"

"Twenty-nine."

"Which means we are the same age in dog years!" Jonathan said, as if this would comfort me about the age difference. But it was wasted. I didn't feel weird at all. Sexy Friendship knows no age.

"In human years, you're both straight up OLD," Bekah said, grinning.

The welcome bell jingled behind me, and a large group of hipster youths took their time filing through the door, letting all the heat out of the restaurant. They shivered spastically as they squeegeed melted snowflakes from their thick-rimmed glasses. From the amount of snow caked to their Doc Martens, they'd trudged through a wintry hellscape to get here.

"Ugh." Bekah threw her head back. "I'll take the bullet, J. Let you lovebirds chat."

With Bekah gone, the night grew intimate fast. Jonathan talked low and leaned in close. He smelled like aftershave, and his hair looked as soft as an alpaca. I wanted to bury my face in his neck and run my fingers through that mane, but I stood strong in my resolve to maintain our Sexy Friendship.

When he laughed and went to touch my hand, I retracted it smoothly;[27] when he asked my deepest darkest secret, I chose my lightest shallowest one (I don't care for Beyoncé);[28] and when he wanted to know about my hopes and dreams, I told him about the recurring dream I have about a panda doing my taxes.[29] I dodged every attempt he made to advance our relationship . . . all except for one. Curiosity got the best of me, and I slipped up and broke Rule #11: Thou Shalt Not Travel Down Past-Relationship Road.

You know Past-Relationship Road: the reminiscent journey you go on with a potential beau where you showcase what you've learned in prior relationships, what you bring to the table, and what crap you won't put up with anymore. Jonathan's

---

27 Sexy Friendship Rule #3: Thou shalt not have physical contact.

28 Sexy Friendship Rule #9: Thou shalt not allow a Sexy Friend into the depths of thy soul.

29 Sexy Friendship Rule #5: Thou shalt not share thy hopes and dreams with thy Sexy Friend.

road consisted of only one serious ex: a bat-shit crazy gal named Leslie.

We sane girls should always be thankful for insane exes because they make normal look amazing by setting the bar low. As long as we don't set our paramours' couches on fire or put Sriracha in their underwear, we look incredible. They're like, "I accidentally spilled coffee in her car, and she didn't poison my dog in retaliation—I think she's the one."

With that said, there is a vital question that needs answered when a crazy ex—or any ex, for that matter—is in the mix: Does he have a picture of her?

Posed eight years ago, that small question could have saved me months of heartbreak and a jail sentence, so listen closely: if he has a picture of her on him, he's crazy for crazy. He may deny it. He may say that he forgot to delete it from his phone or take it out of his wallet: baloney. He still wants her. He may tell you that she is the worst, that she donated all of his clothes to the Nazi Party and insulted his mother's cellulite-infested haunches. Doesn't matter. If he has a picture of her on him, they're going to get married. Run.

However, there is one exception to the picture rule: social media. Emotional distance and creeping? That's my shit. So when Jonathan didn't have a picture (alleluia), I had him sneak out his phone and pull up her picture. Why? Because I was a curious little minx with limited Internet access.

"That's her," he said. It was hard to tell what she looked like with her mouth glued to a beer bong, so I had him flit to an older picture.

CUE WATERFALL OF INSECURITY.

Her long auburn hair cascaded over her huge boobs, and her smile was white like a fresh snowfall. She was one of those girls who didn't need makeup to look awake and alive. God had given her a naturally tan complexion, rosy cheeks, and perfectly tailored eyebrows. As I scanned the photo, her Buddha belly surprised me. HAHA! I guess doing keg stands has its consequences. Suck it, Sexy McPrettyPants!

"Yeah," Jonathan said, taking a shotgun to my jealous pride, "she was pregnant then. She's engaged to the father now, I think."

I recanted all vapid celebration. I had seen pictures of my mom pregnant and, if genetics have anything to do with it, I'll be more Michelin Man than human when I'm expecting. Touché, Hottie McBigKnockers. Touché.

"We met junior year of college in a stats class. We both failed the year before, so we bonded over needing to pass it. We started dating at the end of the semester."

"How long did you date?"

"Five years. The last two were a nightmare, though," he said. "I should've walked away a lot earlier, but when you're in love, you try to make it work."

"What was the breaking point?"

"It was a culmination of things." He paused. "Let me preface by saying that I had my fair share of wild nights in college. I've done Jell-O shots, played beer pong, and dominated Edward Fortyhands. I'm not a prude. But she was an alcoholic. She didn't have her first drink until after college, but once she did, she partied *hard,* and by then I was over the party scene. I wanted to do all the things that I was too poor to do in college, but all she wanted to do was barhop. It didn't help that she was a mean drunk. She tried to fight girls and rope me into fighting guys. It was ugly."

"Did you fight them?"

"I'm not a fighter, but that ticked her off even more. When I finally broke up with her, she slashed my tires, keyed my car, and threw up on my porch repeatedly. I think she meant to ding dong ditch, but she was too drunk."

"Oh my gosh."

"She showed up here a couple times, and we had to call the police." He pulled back his shirt collar where a faded pink line marked his jugular artery. "Scratched the hell out of me."

"Holy sh—" I covered my mouth.

"I had to get a restraining order. When I was younger I thought getting girls would be the hard part of dating, not keeping them away."

"I can safely say I've never drunkenly terrorized an ex."

"That's all I'm looking for in a girl."

My stomach lurched a bit; if Jonathan thought I was the kind of girl he was looking for, he was wrong. I wasn't the girl for him or anyone else.

He smiled, not taking notice of my wave of discomfort. "So, what's your story with your ex? The non-Wikipedia version."

Truthfully, I hadn't thought much about him in the last couple months, and if it were up to me, I never would, but for better or for worse, it was my story so I told it.[30]

Jonathan sat quietly, politely nodding and shaking his head at intervals until the end of the breakup saga when, finally, he spoke. "Not to speak ill of the dead, but what a dick."

Beautiful.

Officer Ramsey walked across the room. "Roads are clear. Get up."

"All right." I turned to Jonathan. "Tonight's been—"

"Hey!" Ramsey pounded the table with his fist. "I didn't say finish your conversation. Put your goddamn coat on, and let's go."

"Sorry, I was just—"

"You were just what? Disobeying a direct order?" He grabbed my coat from the chair and threw it over my head. "Get the fuck up."

"Sorry," I mumbled, pulling the jacket from my eyes. My cheeks burned like coals. Jonathan didn't need to see this.

---

30 Sans Facebook pictures because the only ones left were on his RIP memorial page, which was too depressing to think about.

"I don't give a flying shit if you're sorry." His gaunt cheeks puffed with anger, his green eyes throwing daggers at me. "Get your ass up."

"Officer Ramsey, can I speak to you for a minute?" Jonathan stood up, motioning for Ramsey to move out of earshot.

Ramsey looked around skeptically. "Garcia, keep an eye on her."

I panicked. *What is he doing?*

The shining-armor routine wasn't going to impress me; it was going to get me in trouble. Ramsey was going to report that Jonathan was showing undue interest in me, and I could get kicked out of Decaf for even the appearance of impropriety.

Officer Garcia and I watched their tête-à-tête from the door. I could feel droplets of sweat forming on my hairline like a shiny headband. After a minute, Jonathan left to stack chairs, and Ramsey stomped past us into the snowy parking lot.

The anxiety in my stomach was compounded by the silent car ride. Usually, Ramsey filled the car with NPR and angry ranting, but instead he sat quietly in the passenger seat wringing his hands, looking out the window into the snowy oblivion.

I braced myself as he escorted me to my cell. Jonathan had ticked him off, and, one way or another, I was going to pay for it. The bars passed my face, and the door clicked shut.

Ramsey took a step back and contorted his face. "I'm sorry for what I said." He paused. "Let your boyfriend know."

CHAPTER 34

How Jonathan Met Your Ramsey

"What the hell was that?" I asked Jonathan when my date went to drain his cyst in the bathroom.

"What was what?"

"Don't give me that. You know what: Ramsey, last week. What did you say to him?"

"Ah." He nodded. "I meant to ask, how has he been treating you?"

Good question. The answer: extraordinarily. He said please, bless you, thank you, you're welcome, my pleasure. He even scolded Officer Carmel for making passes at me. "He apologized for what he said to me. What happened? Did you give him a lobotomy?"

"I told him he should rethink how he speaks to you."

"And?"

Officer Ramsey was a tough bastard. I heard that his grandmother, on her deathbed, told him to be a good boy, and he slapped her in the face and stole her car. And her dog. And poisoned the water supply.

"And I told him if he kept talking to you like that, I'd have to tell his wife about his affair."

"WHAT?"

"He brings his wife Jeanette here. She is awesome. She teaches middle school, does mission trips, but she has a fucking blind spot when it comes to that prick Ramsey. He cheats on her. Once a month he brings his side piece here, and even though I can't prove it, she looks underage."

"It could be his daughter," I suggested.

"I saw him get to second base with her last week."

"Oh, probably not his daughter."

"We hope."

I let what he'd told me sink in. "I don't know how I feel about you blackmailing him. It doesn't seem totally ethical to threaten to destroy a man's life by exposing his dirty little secret."

"Guys like Ramsey get off on treating people like crap, and when I saw him talk to you like that . . ." He hesitated. "I didn't have your back before, and I didn't want to make the same mistake again. I'm sorry if I crossed a line."

Jonathan tucked his lips between his teeth, waiting for me to say something.

If I were an Amish girl . . . an Anabaptist churchgoer . . . a Quaker soul, Jonathan's actions would have disgusted me. But I was just a girl . . . standing in front of a boy . . . who extorted an asshole for her. An asshole who, it's worth noting, cheated on a woman who was head over heels for him. I could relate, and for that Ramsey deserved a lifetime of paper cuts full of lemon juice.

"Thank you." I smiled.

All of a sudden, Bekah snuck up behind Jonathan and slammed her hands down on his shoulders. He winced. That had to hurt. Her mitts were large and strong like a milkmaid's.

"Hey, Bekah," he said.

"Did you tell her the good news?" she asked.

Jonathan blushed pink as a panther.

"What good news?"

Bekah looked at Jonathan quizzically. "Why haven't you told her?"

"I was getting to it." He cracked a smile and looked at me. "I got accepted into Henderson-Williams's social policy grad program."

"Congratulations!" I exclaimed way too loudly. Officer Lenny looked my way, pushing his finger to his wrinkled lips. I had nearly forgotten about Jonathan's grad school application. It gave Jonathan nervous sweats talking about it, so we avoided the subject like a mall kiosk. Now he was luminescent with scholarly pride.

Bekah pinched his cheek. "We are so proud of our little graduate student! In a few years, you'll be on the White House's payroll, wining and dining all those Richie Riches, talking to them about healthcare or whatever." She pinched his cheek harder, the blood leaving the skin between her fingers. "Oh yes, you will."

When I got back to Coffee, I threw myself on my lumpy mattress. One rogue spring poked my appendix, but I didn't care. I was imagining Jonathan and me at a gala in DC honoring his work in a prestigious healthcare think-tank. I pictured my sparkly navy dress with a slit up my right leg and his sharp gray suit with a matching navy bow tie. The chandeliers would sparkle like the senators' wives' ostentatious earrings, and the click of high heels would chirp like wild birds. The wine would flow smooth and expensive, and the real estate moguls would excuse themselves to the veranda for cigars. Government officials and celebrities would come up to Jonathan and ask, "Is that your lovely wife shoving shrimp cocktails down her gown?" and he would answer with a coy smile, "No, that's my Sexy Friend, Florence, whom I met whilst she was incarcerated. She's been my biggest inspiration," and those turd flowers would fall silent with jealousy.

When that fantasy ran its course, I reverted to envisioning Officer Ramsey's reaction when Jonathan threatened to expose his shameful double life. From where I'd been standing that day, I could only see the back of Ramsey's head, but it would've have been sweet as honey to see his stoic face fall like Olympus when he realized that he had the losing hand. After all this time, I was glad he'd gotten a taste of what it meant to be at the mercy of someone else.

Suddenly, Officer Ramsey materialized at my cell door. Had he sensed I was gloating over his downfall? His pale green eyes were hard. "Come with me."

Uh boy. There were consequences for Jonathan challenging Ramsey's authority after all.

He escorted me down the darkened hallway, the same hallway he had a hundred times before. I could make out a familiar discolored cinderblock on the left, which meant we were headed to Dr. Sean's office.

Maybe Ramsey tattled on me, and Dr. Sean wanted to talk about Jonathan. That wouldn't be the end of the world; I could explain that Ramsey was being ruder than usual, and that Jonathan, an innocent bystander, had stood up for me.

Then a thought so obvious occurred to me that it stopped me in my tracks. Ramsey pushed me on.

It was late. Too late for Dr. Sean to still be here.

Why was Ramsey taking me to an abandoned office? It was a redundant question. The answer was practically written on the dirty linoleum.

He was going to beat me up just like Ashley all those years ago. But I'd be lucky if I got out of it with only a bruised stomach. She had insulted him, but I—I had put his family life in jeopardy. I was in danger, and I had no way to protect myself. All of the self-defense classes that I never took flashed before my eyes. My heart pounded in my ears as he led me into Sean's office by my cuffs.

I turned toward him and flexed my core, bracing myself for the impact. "Let's get this over with."

Ramsey's thick, bushy eyebrows sank, and he pointed to Dr. Sean's desk.

My throat went to sand. He wasn't going to beat me up; he was going to force himself on me.

WELP, I hadn't killed anyone before, but tonight was as good a night as any. I hoped he kept me handcuffed so I could plead self-defense.

I backed up slowly, never taking my eyes off him. I stopped when I felt the mahogany desk behind me. There was nowhere else to go. I braced for the attack, but Ramsey remained in the doorway and motioned with his chin. "Phone."

An old, black-corded phone lay on Dr. Sean's desk calendar.

He walked out, shutting the door behind him. I looked at the receiver tentatively. I had never been left in a room unsupervised at Coffee. I picked it up. "Hello?"

"Is this Florence?" a man's voice asked. There was chaos in the background: murmured voices, high-pitched beeping, an indecipherable intercom.

"Yes? Who is this?"

"This is Dr. Seidman from Acadia Hospital's emergency department. It is my unfortunate obligation to inform you that your parents were in an accident."

CHAPTER 35

Bad News

My chest caved in, sending my sternum through my heart. Cold sweat ran down my back and the room began to spin, the carpet and walls melding into a sickly blur of brown, green, and beige. I couldn't catch my breath—it was like someone had shoved a vacuum cleaner down my throat and cranked it up to maximum. Somewhere from miles away, Dr. Seidman's voice echoed.

"Hello? Florence?"

I swallowed. "Are . . . are they d—"

"No, they are alive and responsive. I'm happy to say that I don't suspect any brain injury, but I ordered an MRI to confirm. However," he continued, "your father's legs are shattered, and your mother has a serious hip injury. Both have broken ribs and whiplash, but considering the force at which the semi hit them, they're lucky to be alive."

"If they're alive, why aren't *they* calling me?"

"Your mother is in surgery, and your father is heavily sedated. Now, we find that having family support makes a difference in these serious situations, but if you don't have anyone—"

"Give me forty-five minutes, and I'll be there."

"Isn't this"—he cleared his throat awkwardly—"a penitentiary landline?"

I snapped back to reality. "Oh."

"Do you have any family in the area?"

"No, but I'll get someone there," I said robotically and hung up.

When I was a kid, my entire extended family had lived within a few miles of our house, but as years went by, the young ones migrated west and the old ones south, leaving only my parents and me in Maine.[31] But I made the calls anyways.

It was astounding how many of my cousins had unbreakable obligations. Apparently, wedding showers, school plays, and craft shows were more important than family. Even my aunts and uncles were willing to send prayers and flowers, but not to come themselves. They said they weren't comfortable traveling in the snow, but the truth was they were selfish. And if you think I'm being too harsh, let's hit your parents with a semi and see how you feel.

By the grace of God, the black sheep of the family, Uncle Paul, came through. He hadn't made a marriage or sobriety work, but he was packed and ready to go before I hung up the phone. I think black sheep are more prone to acts of sacrifice because they know what it's like to hit rock bottom. They may not be sure what they're doing with their lives, but they know what their purpose is in that moment: to be present for the person who needs it most.

---

31 Yes, that means I'm an only child, you judgmental sibling-haver!

His ex-wives would say that it's easy to play the hero in a pinch, but it doesn't make him a saint, and they'd be right.

But I didn't need a saint. I needed Uncle Paul.

CHAPTER 36

Horrible

- *Replacing my toilet paper with sandpaper*
- *Using Frank's RedHot in my neti pot*
- *Breaking my femur*
- *Sitting on a bed of acid-dipped needles*
- *Listening to John Mayer*
- *Giving birth to a hedgehog*

I wrote an endless list of horrible, painful things to distract myself from the horrible, painful truth: I couldn't be there for my parents. I was trapped behind Coffee's cinderblock walls. At night, instead of being haunted by Her, I was barraged by images of my parents lying in loose fitting hospital gowns, pale as death, ringing for nurses who'd never come.

Weirdly enough, Officer Ramsey was a saving grace during this time. Coffee normally only allowed us one half-hour phone call on Tuesday mornings,[32] but Ramsey took me to Dr. Sean's office every night so I could speak with my parents privately. I could tell by the way he looked over his shoulder that the Warden hadn't given him permission to do this, but I think he fig-

---

32 Monitored and recorded for quality and training purposes.

ured it was worth the risk if it meant staying on my good side, and consequentially, Jonathan's good side.

Still, it wasn't enough. I needed to be with them, and I wasn't. What kind of daughter was I?

"They don't blame you," Jonathan reminded me while my date filled out his evaluation. "You're the reason that your uncle is even there. That was you." His blue eyes searched my face, reading the worry on my forehead.

I avoided his gaze by focusing on the patch of stubble he'd missed while shaving, just under his chin.

"He can't stay with them forever," I said. "Who's going to take them to their doctor's appointments after they're discharged?"

"Hospitals have shuttle services, or sometimes insurance will provide something. They have health insurance, right? They're covered?" Jonathan's social-policy boner was showing.

"Yes, they have insurance."

"Okay." He nodded. "I know it's easier said than done, but you can relax. Your uncle has it covered, and you're doing everything you can."

And for a time, I was marginally comforted.

Their surgeries went well, and for a man who hadn't taken an Advil in ten years, my father was surely appreciating his Vicodin. My mom never complained about the pain, but she did constantly complain that her house was sliding into disarray. Between watching *Judge Judy* and playing rummy, my uncle was derelict in his cleaning duties. *He wiped the counters, sure, but what about the ceiling fans, light fixtures, and floorboards, Florence?!* I encouraged her to rechannel her cabin fever into crocheting. Since then, she had finished three blankets, five hats, and eleven scarves.

My uncle, on the other hand, was thriving in his new care-taking position/dream job. His room and board were taken care of, he was catching up on his shows, and we were deeply indebted to him. He was *loving* it. He was the MVP of our family, and I wasn't shy about telling him so. I secretly hoped that if he felt invaluable and appreciated, he'd stay with them.

AND IT WORKED. He was so happy that he even stuck around to drive them to their physical therapy appointments.

Until he didn't.

Until one morning, he had to meet a friend in Atlanta and left.

His ex-wives were right: great in crises, bad in life. But that's what I signed up for. No more, no less.

I consoled myself by repeating Jonathan's words and using some of Dr. Sean's positive thinking techniques (you don't go through five years of therapy without learning a thing or two). *My parents will get there,* I told myself. *They are insured. Not everyone has transportation; they'll make it work. Worrying about it wouldn't change anything.*

"No one will pick us up," my mother reported over the phone. *Damn Dr. Sean and his BS platitudes.* "The insurance lady said we 'live in the boonies,' and only a UFO would pick us up out here."

"Florence," my dad yelled, "can you hear me?"

"Yes, Dad, you put me on speakerphone—you don't have to shout."

"I got the girl fired," he continued, still yelling. "The UFO girl. I told her boss, and he's gunna fire her. Says she's been a problem for a lot of people."

"Great, Dad, but what are you guys going to do for physical therapy and for groceries?"

"Your mother signed us up for Meals on Wheels. They must fly UFOs to get here."

"Meals on Wheels? You can't! You're too young! That's for people who loaded their dinosaurs onto the Mayflower and signed the Magna Carta."

"Wildly inaccurate," my father mumbled.

"I told you she'd be like this," my mother mumbled back.

"I'm on speakerphone, I can hear you!"

"Don't overreact. We are seniors, technically, and no other place will deliver out here. Goodness forbid we enjoy the country! Anyways, it's only temporary until we can drive again."

"So Meals on Wheels is taking you to PT?"

"No," she answered reluctantly, "we haven't figured that part out yet. We may have to put it off until we can drive."

"Are you kidding? You won't be able to walk, let alone drive, without physical therapy! You're both in wheelchairs for Pete's sake! If you don't go, you're going to heal all mangled!"

"I don't know what you want us to do. If it was once a week, *maybe*, but it's three times a week. *For six weeks.* I'm not putting that on anyone at church."

"What about your friends, Dad?"

"All in Florida this time of year," he grunted.

"Then you have to ask your church friends, Mom. They'd be happy to support you in your time of need! Love your neighbor as yourself, remember?"

"No, no, God will work it out."

"He provided you with an entire church body, use them!"

"It's three days a week for six weeks. Too much to ask," she said decidedly.

"Dad?" I pleaded. "Do something."

"My body's been healing itself for sixty-one years. I'll be fine."

"I can't be—" I stopped myself and heaved a breath. "Mom, please. Call your friends. I couldn't live with myself if you didn't heal well . . . please, do it for me."

There was a long silence. "I'll see what I can do."

CHAPTER 37

Chauffer

"What kind of psychos get in a near-fatal car accident and think they can skip out on intensive physical therapy?" I scrubbed the corner of one of the Domestics' cells.

Rather than making each prisoner responsible for keeping her own space clean, Dr. Sean and the sanitation staff (Greg) had decided that it would be a great idea if, once a week, two prisoners were responsible for cleaning everyone's cells. Supposedly this would encourage bonding, teamwork, and accountability. This week, Lovely Elizabeth and I were the lucky winners.

She wiped sweat off her forehead with her arm, avoiding the yellow rubber gloves on her hands. "Perhaps it's misguided, but it's their attempt not to be a burden. How large is your mother's congregation?"

I stopped scrubbing and counted. "Thirty. It's not a big church."

"Someone will be gracious enough to help. If each person in the congregation transported them once or twice, they could make it to all their appointments."

"That's true." I bit my lip. "I looked up how much it'd cost to Lyft them there and back, and it's insanely expensive. Taxis are even worse. I'd be broke before they were halfway through rehab."

Greg popped by. "I love that I don't have to clean your cells. Especially Gretchen's. How much poop do you have to throw to get committed to a mental hospital?"

"The Warden said he doesn't care as long as she doesn't start eating it. Karen's cell is almost as bad. Her floor is always sticky! Why? Does she spray it down with honey? Coat it with jelly? What is her sticky secret?!"

"Gregory . . ." Lovely Elizabeth stopped scrubbing and sat back on her heels. "We were previously speaking of Florence's parents. They are in need of transportation to their medical appointments. Could you be of assistance?"

Greg looked at me. "They need rides?"

"If my mom can't get her friends to drive them. But don't worry about it, I'll figure it out." Truth be told, I didn't want to ask Greg. It was too big a favor to ask of someone I was trying not to lead on.

"I wish I could help." He bit his lip. "But I can't."

I was taken off guard. Was I vain enough to assume he'd drop everything to help me? Yes, yes I was. Maybe Greg wasn't as in love with me as I thought. I guess that was a win-lose.

"I don't have a license," Greg muttered.

Lovely Elizabeth blushed, averting her eyes. "Excuse me, I shouldn't have assumed."

"You don't have a license?" I asked in disbelief. "How do you get to work?"

"I carpool with the Warden," he said.

"Really," I said skeptically.

"Or, you know, I have a bus pass."

"You never felt the need to be independent and just drive somewhere on a whim?" I looked out the window and felt the pulse of the world calling to me.

"Buses go most places."

I sighed. "Not my parents' house."

Greg looked miserable. "I'm so sorry. If I had known . . . Florence, I would do anything for you. I would drive across the county, across the freakin' ocean for you. You love your parents so much, and I hate that I can't do this for you. Hell, your dad is nicer to me than my own dad is. I know you're disappointed in me. I'm disappointed in me."

"Greg, it's fine. Chill." Maybe Greg was still a little bit in love with me. Lose-lose.

"This sucks. I'm sorry," he added one last time.

"The congregation will resolve it, Florence." Lovely Elizabeth went to give me a pat on the arm, but seemed to remember her rubber plastic gloves, and instead gave me a nudge with her elbow. "Don't fret."

CHAPTER 38

Sexy Friendship

And doggone it, the church folk pulled through—two days a week.

I had to give them credit. The median age of the congregation was seventy-five, and cataracts were spreading like peanut butter, but they were stepping up to the plate. Say what you will about The Church; when they love one another, it's a beautiful thing.

"Two days a week?" Jonathan asked. "That leaves one day not covered."

"They'll have to skip it." I shrugged. "I figure they can just extend their therapy until they've made up for the missed days."

"I can take them," Jonathan said.

I choked on my water. "No, it would be . . . what . . . a forty-five minute drive to their house, then forty-five minutes back here to Acadia Hospital, then forty-five back to their house? That's over two hours of driving, not counting the time their appointments take." I shook my head. "They'll be fine."

"I'm happy to do it."

I shook my head again.

"If you're worried about my driving record, it's clean. I got into a fender bender once, but it wasn't my fault; the guy rear-ended me."

"It's not that. Your work schedule is too unpredictable. I can't afford for you to get called in and miss their appointment."

"I'll take off on their appointment days." He dismissed my concerns with a languid wave of his hand. "Having call-off seniority is the only advantage to working here since undergrad."

I hesitated. "How much would I owe you? What's your rate?"

"Florence, I'm not an Uber."

Something warm and nervous brewed in my stomach. This entire situation was against Sexy Friendship Rules #2 and #7: *Thy Sexy Friend shall never meet thy parents,* and *Thy Sexy Friend shall not give without receiving, lest that put thee in debt to thy Sexy Friend.* I had remained strong thus far, and I wasn't going to compromise now. "I'm going to pay you."

"I won't take it."

"You and I aren't"—I waved my finger like a metronome between us—"I don't do"—I kept metronoming—"you know, like the whole . . ." My finger continued pointing between us. I grabbed the possessed finger with my other hand. This was not going well. "I can't let you take them. Our lives would get intertwined."

"And that would be bad?"

"Yes, very bad. Because as much as we like each other, we don't want to risk this becoming a real relationship."

"We don't?"

"No, because relationships are death machines that rob people of joy and crush their souls," I replied matter-of-factly.

He looked confused. "We've been talking for six months, and my soul doesn't feel too crushed yet."

"Mine neither!" I smiled. "That's how I know our Sexy Friendship has been a success."

"What the hell is a Sexy Friendship?"

"It's us," I said lightly. Inwardly, I was panicking. We had gone months without having this conversation, and I didn't want to have it now. By keeping our Sexy Friendship unspoken, I'd kept it safe, protected. Saying it aloud felt like exposure. It gave Jonathan a choice: go along with it or walk away.

"The best way I can explain it is that we have undeniable chemistry and enjoy each other's company, but we don't have to deal with all the shit that comes with relationships."

"So friends with benefits?" he asked, amused.

"Well, without the benefits . . . obviously," I said nervously. "I know it seems sort of old fashioned, but if we had . . . *benefits*, I would inevitably develop feelings for you or vice versa, and it would get messy."

"For the record, I'd be willing to deal with relationship shit if it was with you. Like I said before, I already have feelings for you."

This really wasn't going well.

"I'm not willing to ruin what we have," I replied stubbornly. "The moment that we try to be anything more than flirty, we're destined for failure. I don't want that."

He stayed quiet.

"Now you see why I can't let you drive them."

Jonathan sat forward, sliding his elbows to his knees. "Ah, Florence." He rubbed his scruffy face; he had let his beard grow out in the last few weeks. "Why don't I drive them, as a friend?" His eyes met mine. "Nothing romantic."

"Yeah?"

"Yeah. Friends do favors for each other all the time. I helped my friend Rob move apartments, and I covered a shift for Bekah before she left for Spain. It's normal for a friend to help out another friend."

"A friend favor?" I clarified hesitantly.

"If that's what you want."

"That would be—yes, that would be perfect," I said with relief.

Ironically, Jonathan agreeing to do me a "friend favor" was the first time that I considered dating him.

Don't worry, I recognized it for what it was: reverse psychology. By not pushing the dating issue, he made me want to date him. Jonathan wasn't doing it on purpose, from what I could tell, but purposeful or not, it was an effective tactic. If I were a novice, I'd have caved—would've asked him out right then and there, but I was a grown woman with a bank account and a vague understanding of the Dewey decimal system! I wasn't going to be tricked into dating by some reverse psychology witchcraft. I was better than that!

Jonathan was a rose—beautiful and alluring, yes, but all roses have thorns. It's merely a consequence of being a lovely, fragrant rose. Lo, I had been an entranced gardener in past; I was wiser now. I knew enough to observe his beauty, breathe in his sweet bouquet, but let him be. I needn't get entangled in his thorns to enjoy him.

He was good though; I'll give him that. Damn good.

CHAPTER 39

Intensity

Susie the Strangler and I picked fresh green cucumbers from the small greenhouse sustained in the east wing of the prison. The sun shone through the greenhouse windows, heating up the saturated air, and I instantly began sweating. My forehead dripped as I bent down to wrangle with the assorted vegetables. Nothing thrived as well as the cucumbers, but the tomatoes tried their best, though they were lopsided and a little ugly. The red peppers and onions were an even sadder sight, but the chefs needed some for a salad, so those came with us too. Vegetable-picking never took as long as other chores, so we dropped off the fruits of our labor and loaded up our blue lunch trays before the other prisoners got out. The chefs asked if we wanted to wait for the salad to be ready. We laughed. Did we look like rabbits?

"Let me get this straight: he is willing to drive your parents to physical therapy every week and you *reject* him? I'm starting to think you don't got the sense God gave a goose."

"I'm going to send him an edible arrangement, is that better?"

"Baby girl, that's worse and you know it!"

"Yeah." I sighed. "But Jonathan being awesome doesn't negate the fact that relationships are the worst. Everyone I ever dated did something romantic for me at some point. Jonathan could easily be part of the pattern."

"Driving gimpy parents ain't romantic, it's—"

"Dutiful? Boy Scout-ish?"

"Kindhearted."

I snorted. "I'm sure Jeffrey Dahmer had his good days."

"Sounds like Jonathan's been kind for a lot of days . . ."

"So?"

"He's your person, Florence!" she said, exasperated. "He's your guy!"

I rolled my eyes. "My *soul mate*?"

She waved her hand. "Soul mate business is malarkey. Phil and I have been married thirty-six years. We stick together because we want to, not because 'the universe' is forcing us. We decided to make it work, so it does."

"And if one person isn't willing to make it work?"

"You've seen how that goes, darlin'." She smiled weakly. "But, I'm tellin' you, the most interestin' woman in the world could walk past Phil, and it wouldn't matter a lick. He'd find her lovely, and even get to talkin' to her, but even the Queen of Sheba couldn't change the fact that he's mine through and through. Anything less than that ain't love."

"I wish I could be so confident about someone."

"You could be, if you let yourself."

The room began to fill with noise, prisoners, and guards. Greg snuck in among them. I had never noticed that his blue jumpsuit was so similar to our orange ones. It buttoned up the middle like ours, but his had pockets that were always stuffed with cleaning rags. He had the build of an upright salamander, but when his pockets were full, it made him look like a stick with birthing hips.

Feminist Lorraine went to sit next to me, but he hip-checked her out of the way. And slammed a McDonald's cup on the table. "Happy St. Patrick's Day!"

"It's mid-April," I said.

"Close enough."

"Where did you even get that?" Susie the Strangler asked.

"I have my methods," he said quickly. "So what's up, buttercup?"

I slurped down my Shamrock Shake. "Another day in paradise."

"You got that right." Greg took a French fry off my tray and shoved it into his mouth. "How are your parents doing?"

"Great, from what they tell me. They're tired a lot, but I think the medication makes them drowsy."

"Are they surviving the car rides?" he asked nonchalantly. "They getting along with Jared or whatever his name is?"

And there it was. Part of me regretted telling him about their transportation arrangements, but I didn't want to lie about it. I had no reason to lie about it! There was nothing scandalous going on, and even if there was, so what?

"His name is *Jonathan*. And they haven't said much about him, actually."

I wasn't being coy; it was the truth. A suspicious, suspicious truth. My mother, the master of interrogation, hadn't inquired once about Jonathan. A handsome man showed up at their door, and there was no curiosity? He could've been an escort I hired, for all she knew! But still, no questions? It was maddening.

Greg laughed wryly. "There probably isn't much to say; he's a waiter. What is he going to talk about? Tables and food and stuff?"

Susie the Strangler rolled her eyes. "Says the janitor."

"Hey, I don't see you guys complaining when I sneak you snacks."

"You've been slacking!" I smirked, slamming down my Shamrock Shake. "I've been craving Ritz crackers for a week. Afraid the Warden is going to catch you?"

"Screw the Warden, I'm not scared of him." He waved a hand dismissively. "The store only has the reduced-fat ones, and last August when I gave you reduced-fat vanilla wafers, you pelted me in the face with them."

"In my defense, how gross is reduced fat?"

"Straight-up cardboard. If I'm going to lose weight, I'm gunna eat a lot of fast food then take a giant poop."

"Come on, man."

"After seeing whatever this is, I kinda have to take a dump." He pointed to the yellow sludge on my tray.

"It's corn chowder." I grimaced.

"Seriously, I want to drop a deuce just looking at it."

"Stop," Yosemite Karen said from the end of the table. "I'm trying to eat."

He opened his mouth to retort, but the Warden emerged from the east wing and began stomping through the cafeteria. For all his tough talk, Greg disappeared in record time.

"Never thought I would be thankful for that tub of lard," Yosemite Karen said, eying the Warden.

"Gregory is absurd." Lovely Elizabeth dabbed the corner of her mouth with her perfectly folded napkin. "He does not respect your relationship with Jonathan. He must be aware how petty he appears when he disparages him so."

"Greg's gotta know that he doesn't stand a chance with you," Nympho Yvette said. "You're a badass frizzy-haired queen, and he's a skinny dude who talks about poop." She stroked my face with the back of her hand. "Such a goddess cannot lie with a mortal man."

"A goddess?" I repeated skeptically. "Goddesses don't wear orange, Yvette. And I'm not better than him. He was one of my first friends here. Actually, he was my first friend here."

I remembered my first encounter with Greg. I had just gotten to Coffee, and as I was lying in my bed, hoping I'd only have to stare at the ceiling for a year, he knocked on my cell door. He introduced himself and gave me the inside scoop: which guards were nice, which prisoners seemed cool, and what food to avoid. Then he smiled and said, "Chin up, you'll do fine here."

He made me feel comfortable in a strange place, and for that I would always be grateful.

"Part of me wants to like him," I admitted. "He obviously means well, but I just don't feel that way. He's like a little brother to me."

One of the Domestics shuffled over. "I've always thought he was creepy."

"No, come on." Just because I didn't want to date Greg didn't mean I wanted others to trash him. "He's just a little, you know, awkward."

"I've always gotten majorly weird vibes from him," First Lady Abigail called from down the table.

"Are we talking about Greg?" Feminist Lorraine asked.

"Obviously," Susie the Strangler and Yosemite Karen replied in unison.

"You all think he's creepy?" I asked.

Susie the Strangler wiped crumbs off her jumpsuit. "Maybe creepy is too strong a word. He's *intense*, about you mostly."

I thought back to his over-the-top apology about not being able to drive my parents to their appointments.

"*Super* intense." Yosemite Karen smiled smugly. "I mean, you can't blame the guy. He's got a mediocre job, and the only women he sees are us. Kim clearly isn't going to give him any, so Florence is debatably the next hottest option."

Hot-Rod Kim nodded from the end of the table. She never got involved in drama, but evidently she appreciated the shout-out.

Yosemite Karen stretched her arms over her head. "I've always thought Greg was a desperate little twerp."

I frowned. "He's a kid with a crush. Don't be a jerk."

"What is he going to do without his precious Flo?"

"Don't. Be. A. Jerk," I repeated, glaring. "He's still a human being."

"He'll be fine." Susie the Strangler wrapped me in a hug. "I would promise to be his shoulder to cry on, but—"

"We gunna be free, bitches!" Nympho Yvette high-fived Susie the Strangler, Feminist Lorraine, and Lovely Elizabeth. She put her palm in my face. "High-five me if you're done worrying about Greg and excited to get out of here!"

I hesitated, but Greg was a big boy. He'd be fine.

I high-fived her.

CHAPTER 40

Flirtation: Population: 2

"Wow." Jonathan gaped. "You look beautiful tonight."

"Stop."

"Give us a spin!" he insisted.

"No, the guards will tase me!"

"Worth it, you look awesome."

Admittedly, I did look awesome. My outfit was one of the more flattering ones in Coffee's arsenal: a white swoop-neck shirt with a matching white-trimmed navy blue skirt. It wasn't that impressive, but it *was* less horrifying than the others. I had the vague sense that some rich heiress wore it to a yacht christening, then donated it for the tax deduction.

"Would I be a bad Sexy Friend if I told you that I want to kiss you?"

"Yes." I grinned. "That's against Sexy Friendship Rule #4: Thou Shalt Not Talk about Kissing."

"You prefer 'necking'?"

"Ew, Jonathan."

"Fine. Can I at least tell you that I've thought about showing you off to my friends and family?"

I took a second to think about it. "There's no rule against that, I suppose. Which technically means that I can admit that I've thought about us cuddling, eating blueberry pancakes, and binge-watching *Parks and Rec.*"

"Sounds amazing." He cleared his throat. "Sorry, I mean, 'What a relief that we're Sexy Friends who will never do anything like that ever. God bless Sexy Friendship.'"

Yeah, yeah, I can hear your dry heaving from here. I know, we were gross and flirty and lame, but that's how it had been since we had made our Sexy Friendship official. I had expected things to get weird or for him to get mopey, but to my relief he had a very tongue-in-cheek approach to the whole thing. So keep your dry heaving to yourself! I'd take lame and flirty over him being a dung beetle about it.

"Before I forget, your mom wants me to bring her to Coffee tomorrow."

"Really?" I frowned. "I figured she would die before 'imposing' on you."

"She misses you," he said kindly.

I missed her too. It had been over two months since the accident. Their car was totaled, they were homebound, and even when my Uncle Paul was around, he hadn't brought them to visit. He tried, once. Things went smoothly until he tried to lift my mother into the car, which ended with her in excruciating pain and my father cursing prolifically on her behalf. From then on, Uncle Paul refused to transport them anywhere except for the hospital.

So my only communication with my parents was via phone and through Jonathan, who was my eyes and ears, telling me the truth about their hard days and how they were actually doing.

"Is my dad coming too?"

"She didn't say. You're cool with me bringing her last minute though?"

"Absolutely." I paused, then grinned. "Does that mean that I get to see you outside of a Seminar?"

"You do." He grinned back. "It's been awhile, huh?"

"You'll have to try to control yourself. I can't have you flirting with me in front of my mom, Sexy Friend."

He chuckled, leaned down, and breathily whispered in my ear, "I promise it will be brief and completely un-erotic."

Goosebumps rose up my neck and down my thighs. I tried to come up with a cunning response, but my brain was like, "Hormones, called away on business LOL, k byeeee." So I nodded, hoping he couldn't hear my heart hammering in my chest.

CHAPTER 41

Advice

At 8:00 a.m. the next day, the Decafers were sequestered in an empty conference room that smelled of pencil shavings and construction paper. The air tasted stale, and the furniture looked to be donated school memorabilia: desks with lovers' names etched in the wood; an antique overhead projector collecting dust in the corner; and a rickety podium that wobbled as a chipper, blonde, pregnant woman leaned against it. The blonde wasn't donated; she was Leslie, the career advisor brought in by Dr. Sean to usher us into the workforce. With her sing-songy voice and blinding white smile, she promised us that with her help and our God-given talents, there were jobs out there for us.

She went around the pseudo-classroom, beginning with Nympho Yvette. In case you forgot, Nympho Yvette was a nurse's aide who was convicted of sexing her patients to death. *Cooter Dangereux.* Supposedly, Leslie had found several women's hospitals and nursing homes that were willing to hire Nympho Yvette if she promised not to bang the patients. She seemed put off by the idea of limiting her sex options, but Leslie reminded her that mixing work and pleasure was never a good idea. Nympho Yvette grudgingly agreed, took the applications, and began filling them out.

Leslie turned her attention to Lovely Elizabeth—and practically glowed. She gushed that she had never seen a prisoner in such high demand. Apparently, Lovely Elizabeth was a celebrity in the floral community, and several florists had begun a bidding war over her without her knowledge. By the way Leslie's eyes bulged, Lovely Elizabeth was about to make *beaucoup bucks.* Lovely Elizabeth blushed profusely, but smiled in spite of herself.

You go girl, I thought. If anyone deserved it, it was her.

Susie the Strangler and Feminist Lorraine were next, but they had no need of Leslie's services. Susie the Strangler was a retired schoolteacher, and Feminist Lorraine was a catering entrepreneur, a "self-made woman," as she put it. No matter how she spun it, it made me a little sick to think her patrons wouldn't know about her *quiche a la castration.*

The remainder of Leslie's time was devoted to yours truly. She rubbed her big pregnant belly, and more or less suggested that no one wants a murderer holding their precious baby. She said that she tried—*really, truly tried*—to find a reputable childcare facility that would consider me, but there was nothing. No one would hire an ex-con to watch their child. Her best advice was to go back to school and explore my passions. When I informed her that children were and are my passion (hence my degree in child development), her pink lips pouted.

Would you be interested in writing children's books? No, can't write.

How about making children's clothing? No, can't sew.

What about recording lullabies for babies? No, can't sing.

Then she suggested finding a new passion. Heating and cooling?

Leslie's ill tidings weren't a surprise, but they felt unfair. I wasn't even accused of killing a child! My Childline clearance was spotless! Why did they think I'd pose a threat? Just because children can be unruly and nerve-grating, possibly causing someone with impulse-control issues to inevitably break? Well . . . okay . . . yeah . . . I get that. But I didn't have impulse-control issues and I never killed anyone!

In a perfect world, I'd go to law school and clear my wrongful conviction. But this wasn't *Law and Order*—this was real life, and in real life, Florence falls asleep reading law books.

After Leslie and her baby bump were done feeding on my broken dreams, I went with the other prisoners to the visitation room. I dragged my hands over my hair to tame my brown mane, or maybe to wipe off the shame and disappointment of the last hour; either way, it was useless. The flyaways popped back up, unfazed, and I still felt crummy.

Susie the Strangler's husband Phil was first through the door, as always—he was such a dad, with his ill-fitting jeans and slightly too large polo shirt. He looked tired today. Getting their son ready for college couldn't be easy alone. Susie the Strangler stood up and hugged him. The way they closed their eyes to the world, securing the moment between them, made me heady like I'd huffed something lovely and strong.

I heard a wheelchair *clunk-clunk* over the steel lip of a doorway, and looked over to see Jonathan pushing my smiling mother, who waved at me like Kate Middleton—royalty on wheels. The combination of the two welcome sights had me jumping out of my seat. Before I knew it, I was clinging to my mom. *She's alive, she's okay, she's with me.*

I kissed her on the cheek. "No dad?"

"He's at home. I wanted a little mother/daughter time." She reached up to touch my cheek. Her hand was warm, but frailer than I remembered.

I looked up at Jonathan. His smile was warm like sand and bright like the day. Without thinking, I hugged him. Sexy Friendship Rule # Whatever broken. I entered into his warm, soft insulation. His strong arms rested on my shoulders, my temple against his chest. I breathed him in, savoring his smell. It was different than my ex's natural vanilla scent; it was earthy and crisp like an autumn breeze.

Suddenly, hands came between us. "No hugging, contraband risk." I rolled my eyes at Officer Braeden. He was a newbie, clearly trained by Officer Ramsey. Soon he'd take a chill pill and realize that they searched us before we went back to our cells, so nothing was getting in.

I cleared my throat and returned to my seat. *Mom probably feels weird about our PDA*, I thought. But if she did, she didn't let on. She was watching Gretchen whispering to her sister, most likely scheming world domination.

"I'm going to wait outside," Jonathan said, with an apologetic smile. It was okay. I preferred our non-prison visiting arrangement. It kept Jonathan separate from this world.

He knelt next to my mom's wheelchair. "They'll wheel you out to the parking lot. Meet you out there." She patted his hand, which was resting on her shoulder; I hadn't even noticed it there.

Seeing the exchange made me realize that they had gotten to know each other apart from me. For the last five weeks, they'd had conversations atop heated seats and seen sights through the same windshield. It was a strange relief. My parents wouldn't need me to explain who Jonathan was. They already knew, for better or worse. I wondered if they knew about his abusive father, his superhero mother, his sister Jenn, his grad program in the fall, or his days at The Open Door. Did they delve deep, or was it all shallow hellos and goodbyes?

My mom wheeled herself closer to the table. Our knees knocked as she pulled on the chair's wheel lock. "Remember when I said, 'This too shall pass?'" She squeezed my hand. "It's passing."

"You're almost done with PT."

"And you only have a couple months left."

"Even less." I smiled. "Can't wait to sleep in my own bed."

She raised a hand to her forehead and laughed. "Don't get me started on that bed. I keep having to wash the comforter, because Rusty has taken a liking to sleeping there during the day. It is *covered* in fur." I thought of Charlie Gibson, the loving old Great Dane my ex and I had shared, but I didn't feel the wave of sadness I normally did. "I miss having a dog."

"You should get one, then," my mom said casually.

I eyed her suspiciously. She was famous for telling people that dogs were a huge responsibility, the heaviest of all burdens. "*You* think I should get a dog? Even though I don't have my own place or a job?"

"You'll live with us until you're back on your feet, and you'll have time to train a puppy while you look for work."

"Is Dad dying?" I asked. "Why are you being so weirdly nice?"

She jerked her head back. "Weirdly nice?! Dad's not dying, and neither am I, thanks for asking. I think you deserve some joy in your life, is all. After everything you've gone through, I thought a puppy might give you some comfort during the hard transition."

"Oh." In some ways I was a twenty-nine-year-old woman, and in other ways I was a bratty sixteen-year-old with a *Keep Out* sign on my door. "A puppy would be incredible."

"Rochelle's daughter would like it too, I'm sure," she said.

"Rochelle's daughter?"

"If you're interested," she prefaced. "Rochelle needs someone to watch her daughter Jodi during the week. Just to make sure she gets off the bus, gets her homework done, and gets to gymnastics. It's not a dream job, but it'll hold you over. Rochelle's aware of your record, but she's known you since you were born, and she trusts you."

More like she was desperate and couldn't afford daycare, but beggars can't be choosers. "Would I get paid?"

"Yes, sweetheart—you're a little old for unpaid internships."[33]

The low tide of relief that had been lapping at my toes rose, immersed me. I would have a job with kids. A paying job with kids. It felt like an answer to an unspoken prayer. "Is that why you came? You wanted to tell me in person?"

Her cheeks turned crimson. "Well, not exactly."

I should've known a puppy and a job were buttering me up for the real news. The bad news. "What is it?"

"It's about Jonathan." She took a sharp breath. "I want you to hear me out."

Oh no. He's a serial killer and she found a body in his backseat. WHY, Zodiac Killer? WHYYY???? I managed a nod.

"I haven't said anything in case I was wrong, but . . ." She took an agonizingly long breath. "I believe Jonathan has feelings for you."

"Oh."

"He has done his best to keep things between you two private, but he can't keep it out of his voice. Your father thinks I'm jumping to conclusions, but after seeing you two together, I think you care for him too."

---

33 Shout-out to the millennial reality!

I opened my mouth, but she put up her hand to stop me. "I debated whether or not to say anything to you. Talking about love is different than teasing about a crush, and you're an adult—a woman stronger than I was at your age. It's just . . . you've been forced to develop tough skin to get through everything. No one faults you for surviving, but it's time to thrive. You have so much love to give, if you let yourself."

"You think I'm not letting myself?"

"When I asked about the *nature* of your relationship, he said something about a 'Sexy Friendship.' It sounded more like your idea than his."

Welp, the cat was out of the bag.

I should've been mad at Jonathan for tattling, but more than anything, I was fascinated at how contrived "Sexy Friendship" sounded coming out of my mom's mouth: like talking about an imaginary friend.

"You are old enough to make your own romantic decisions, but I'd hate to see you rob yourself of a good thing. Jonathan has a good heart, and has generously carted us around to our appointments and errands and even out to dinner when we were absolutely stir-crazy."

"He did?" Jonathan hadn't told me about any extra "carting." I felt a lump form in my throat.

"Thought you were Team Greg," I tried to joke.

"I only pushed for him because I thought you were being stubborn about your feelings, but now that I've seen you with

Jonathan . . ." She shrugged. "I don't care who you end up with, as long as they treat you right and you're happy."

"I don't think my judgment can be trusted. Last time I thought I was happy, he left me for Her."

"Just because you dated an asshole doesn't mean you've lost all credibility."

I burst out laughing; I had never heard her swear before. "Language!"

"I'm serious! We've all dated *assholes*," she whispered. "Your father dated a girl who bit him when she was angry for goodness sake! Now he's with me, and I only bite when it's fun."

"Mom!"

"All I'm saying is that everyone dates someone who isn't right for them; it doesn't mean you won't get it right the next time."

She had a point. A majority of happy couples had crummy exes. The difference between them and me was that they got over it.

"Do you think Jonathan would still want to . . . you know . . ."

She smirked. "He's not sitting in the parking lot because he wants to be with *me*."

CHAPTER 42

Giving In

"There are tons of reasons people don't want to date: fear of commitment, fear of intimacy, fear of the opposite sex. You've got polygamists who won't settle down, feminists who hate patriarchal institutions, domestic abuse survivors who are determined not to be re-victimized. All of them are valid reasons, but none are mine." I took a deep breath. "I think I was afraid Jonathan would be like my ex. That he'd fall into someone else's arms and leave me in the same mess as before."

Dr. Sean nodded patiently.

"But it's ludicrous to think that Jonathan is like my ex! He not only drove my parents hundreds of miles to and from the doctor's, but he drove them to errands and stuff. Oh yeah, I forgot to tell you that Jonathan drove my parents all over the fucking place, and not even for the brownie points! Can you imagine the kind of brownie points he could have earned! GERMAN CHOCOLATE RED VELVET CREAM CHEESE BROWNIE POINTS!"

"Why are you telling me this?" Dr. Sean asked.

"Because I like Jonathan. Like, for real, let's-go-on-dates-and-cuddle-and-kiss-and-have-inside-jokes-and-share-French-fries-and-milkshakes-and-go-to-family-fuctions-and-call-each-other-on-the-way-home-from-work like him. I'm going to tell him so, but there's someone else who needs to know first."

"Greg."

"Yes, which is why I came to you with the most private information in my life." Well, okay, that was a lie. I didn't exactly give him the incriminating details of where I met Jonathan, but he knew the basics. "There is a *slight* chance Greg will be heartbroken, and I'd like someone around to look out for him. I want you to make sure he doesn't get too depressed."

"Why tell him at all? You tend to avoid uncomfortable conversations."

Have I ever mentioned that I'm shitty at emotions? Dr. Sean has.

"He made me promise."

The good doctor leaned back in his chair and nodded. "Thank you for confiding in me about this. I'll keep my eye on Greg, and I hope things go well with Jonathan. For what it's worth, your perspective on relationships appears to have grown healthier over the years. As a professional, it's encouraging when you can see progress in a patient. On a personal note, I'm happy to see you exploring something new."

"Thanks," I said. "Any advice on how to break it to Greg?"

"Keep it short and sweet." He leaned forward, resting his chin on his fist. "And don't apologize. I suspect Greg can become manipulative when he doesn't get his own way. You've got nothing to be sorry for. Don't let him guilt-trip you."

I nodded. "Roger that."

CHAPTER 43

Putting On My Big-Girl Pants

A basketball court full of dead robins heralded the first warm spring day. The black billows from the chemical plant interrupted the robin-egg blue sky, a few blades of grass peeked through the cracks on free-throw line, and the wild tulips leisurely stretched their red and yellow petals outside the fence. The weather was perfect. Unfortunately, that meant my allergies reappeared in all their glory. My nose glowed red like Rudolph's, and my bloodshot eyes produced top-of-the-line eye goop. In short, I looked like I was on ragweed-laced heroin.

Stepping over a dead bird, Greg greeted me with all the tact he was capable of. "Holy crap! You look terrible! Are you sick?"

"No, I'm just not wearing any makeup," I said sarcastically.

"Oh, well"—he stepped onto his soapbox—"girls wear too much makeup nowadays. Barbie isn't real, so why does everyone try to look like her? I prefer au naturel."

"Right," I said, half-listening through my fishbowl ears. "You implied I looked terminal. Guys are into that, right? No commitment, fancy Make-A-Wish vacations?"

"You are *drop-dead* gorgeous."

"Greg, we gotta talk."

"Me first! I'm going to quit," he said brightly. "Once you leave. I'm quitting Coffee. It'll be boring without you here, so I'm gunna widen my horizons or whatever."

I tried to rub the headache from my temples. "Cool. Get. A. License."

"If I had the right driving teacher, I would." He smiled slyly.

"I know one." I smiled back. *Her name is Ethel, she's been a driving instructor for twenty-two years, and she too will not be having sex with you.* "What do you even do with your time if you aren't driving places?"

"I'm either here bothering you or at home thinking about bothering you." He laughed. "What can I say? You take up a lot of my time."

Sadly, I believed his world was that small. Maybe that's why I had never been attracted to him. Jonathan had friends, dreams, and passions, but Greg only had me. I could think of no duller hobby.

"I need to tell you something," I said, too loudly. I just wanted to get this over with.

He made a cross with his fingers. "Is it that you're contagious?"

"I am going to date Jonathan."

When Greg's face didn't register anything, I continued slowly, "I told you that if I ever changed my mind about him, I'd give you a heads up ... so ... heads up."

Greg's face remained unchanged. I could almost hear his mind gears turning, trying to process this new bit of information. When he came to, he looked at me. "You don't date."

"Things changed."

"Why?" he scoffed. "Because he gave you roses or something?"

"No." I wiped my runny nose on my sleeve. "I'm allergic to roses."

"I know that, but does *he*?"

I shrugged. "I don't know."

"Well, does he know your favorite food is iced coffee, or that you hate bowling? Does he know the reason that you didn't frame your diploma is because you lost it in a poker game? Does he know that you love pigs? Does he know you at all?"

Heat filled my face. "He doesn't know everything about me, but that's what dating's for—to learn that stuff."

"What if he finds out that stuff, and doesn't like you?"

I ground my teeth—Greg was trying to tap into my insecurities, but I wasn't backing down. "It's a risk I'll have to take."

"But I know everything about you already! I know you used to crochet with your mom, you love Seth Rogan, and you hate John Mayer. I know you'd rather go to a lake than a beach, you're always cold—which is why your sad-mood drink is hot chocolate—and you love *National Geographic*."

He was right, he knew a lot about me—half of those things I didn't even remember telling him—but he'd had five years to get to know me. I'd known Jonathan for less than a year; he wasn't going to be a Florence encyclopedia yet. "What's your point, Greg?"

"You can't date him, Flo! You've spent years saying, 'Relationships are the devil,' and now you're going to date this complete stranger? You don't even know him, and all of a sudden, you're losing who you are!"

"You make it sound like I'm joining a cult! I—" I stopped myself. Dr. Sean was right. I had nothing to be sorry for. "I'm not apologizing. I like Jonathan, and I'm going to date him."

Greg stared back at me, frozen in thought or prayer or catatonia. Ten seconds, ten unbearable seconds. Then he blinked and shook his head. "You're right, I was being an ass."

Was this manipulation or sincerity? "Yeah?"

"Yes, I'm sorry. I'm an idiot. You are amazing, and even though I'm pretty convinced that no one is good enough for you, it can't hurt to see if this Jonathan guy is worthy."

I put the back of my hand to his forehead. "You feeling all right?"

"I'm fine." He grinned and swatted my hand away. "Like I said before, sometimes it takes time for my guy brain to totally get it. Plus, if Jonathan changed *your* mind about dating, he must be a miracle worker."

"I've been known to have a slight stubborn streak." I smirked.

"It's easier to turn water into wine than to convince you of anything. Remember two years ago, when you were sure that C.S. Lewis wrote *The Hobbit*? I brought in three different copies, and you still didn't believe me! It took like five Google searches for you to finally admit you were wrong. Stubborn doesn't begin to cover it."

I picked a tulip from the edge of the fence and smelled it. "I prefer *discerning*. And I would say that it's one of my best qualities."

"Let's hope Jonathan thinks so too. God forbid he has to prove that *Harry Potter* was written by J.K. Rowling."

I threw the tulip at his head. Secretly, I had never been more thankful for Greg. He could've backslid into self-pity and misery, but he chose our friendship instead. He might have been the one with the insanely good memory, but I wouldn't forget this.

CHAPTER 44

Reverse, Reverse

What the hell just happened? One minute, I was ducking into the undercover police car, excited to proclaim my ~~love~~ like for Jonathan, and the next I was standing outside of The Open Door, ready to sabotage any possibility of a relationship.

Per usual, Officer Carmel had complained about his wife the whole car ride. He whined that she was annoying, prudish, and [insert other tiresome misogynistic bullshit]. It was run-of-the-mill conversation as far as I was concerned, the same things I had been forced to eavesdrop on every day. Officer Carmel then nonchalantly mentioned he was going to find someone to fill the "banging void" in his life. He went on and on about how things had gotten boring with his wife. How every day they got up, ate breakfast with the kid, went to work, got home, ate dinner with the kid, put the kid to bed, had sex (only TWICE a week, that vagina-hoarder!), and went to sleep. Every day with her was the same, he complained. He felt trapped.

The women he had seen on dating websites, on the other hand, were fun and new and sexy and full of life! They didn't have to-do lists for him! They weren't slaves to routine! Those women, they were the rush he was looking for!

I was horrified. Not because Carmel had been my male role model. He was a horny Garbage Pail Kid, and I expected nothing better from him. What horrified me was that I had finally pinpointed the real reason I was terrified of dating. I wasn't afraid that Jonathan would turn into my ex; I was afraid of Her. Of Her and all the women like Her. She and the Other Women who weren't boring, who lived lives of adventure, and who proved that the grass was truly greener on the other side.

I couldn't compete with that if I tried.

Because I *had* tried, and I had lost.

I wouldn't put myself through that again. Would you? I mean, picture it: You're a wife and mother of one, two . . . let's say three kids. You and your family are eating lunch in the park under a shady tree when She walks by. She's in a sundress, holding an ice cream cone, smelling feminine and alluring. You, on the other hand, are clad in shorts and a T-shirt because you've got to chase kids around and dresses are impractical. *Do I smell feminine and alluring?* you ask. Hell no. You smell like spit-up and wet wipes.

All it takes is a smile—one small, coy smile in your husband's direction—to plant the seed that there is a better life outside of school pickups, household chores, and marriage logistics. He could drop you and your little ones like a one-night stand and pursue a life with this Better Higher Being.

I was no match for that.

I was one of those "normal girls," not the Beautiful, Intriguing Vixen who could keep a man's attention infinitely. I was the kind of girl who bails on plans when it's snowing, who eats dairy even though she's lactose intolerant, and who lies about being bilingual on job applications. I was the type who needed caffeine to function, had bad handwriting, and was not particularly light-hearted when bad things happened. I could not hold a candle to Her and Her Beautiful Cronies.

It was too late to go back to being Sexy Friends with Jonathan, now that I had admitted to myself that I liked him. The priority now was figuring out how to have him in my life without it heading down the dating track again. Then it came to me.

FRIENDSHIP. Good old-fashioned friendship.

By the time my feet touched The Open Door's rain-drenched parking lot, I had made the decision. We needed to revert to friendship as quickly and seamlessly as possible, for both our sakes.

My hands were sweating and my stomach churned, but it was settled: Jonathan was dead to me romantically.

Cool beans.

CHAPTER 45

Operation Friend Zone

Brad, the recruiter for Cherries Gentlemen's Club, shook my hand. His reputation preceded him; he was known as a shark who preyed on women with poor family lives for the pleasure of men who wore thin sweatpants and gold chains. A tuft of white chest hair peeked out of his purple button-up as he scanned the room for recruits. According to the other Decafers, he was a reasonable businessman who wouldn't waste energy trying to recruit me once I told him I wasn't interested. Nothing could get me to swing around a pole. Except for tequila. But that was one time.

Our waiter materialized to take our order. My butt cheeks clenched faster than a cheetah on Adderall. It was Jonathan. Jonathan was our waiter. But it was fine. Totally fine. Yep, fine. Fine. Fine. Fine. Making him dead to me was going to be a piece of cake.

"Hi, Florence." He smiled. "What can I get you to drink?"

"Gin," my subconscious ordered. Both Brad and Jonathan shot me speculative looks. "'Ger ale," I said, recovering smoothly. "Ginger ale."

"And you, sir?" Jonathan asked. I stared at the backs of his hands; blood surged hot beneath his skin, making his manly veins bulge. Can hands turn one on? Because I was there. Why couldn't he have paper-thin witch hands with hairy moles and liver spots? Was that too much to ask?

"Water, please." Brad patted his belly. "I'm trying to cut out sugars."

"I'll be right back with that." Jonathan flashed me a perfect white smile. *Be snaggletooth, you gorgeous son of a bitch!*

A half-eaten salad and few more increasingly awkward encounters with Jonathan later, Brad's phone rang. From the crying, it sounded like a high school girl just found a way to spite her parents. Screw them and their ten o'clock curfew! He excused himself, and continued the call outside.

"Hey." Jonathan knelt next to the table, throwing off airs. His intimate tone only strengthened my resolve to kibosh it. I didn't need a guy who I had stuff in common with to take that affectionate tone with me. WHAT WAS HIS PROBLEM?

With slight condescension, I commenced my mission to cut him off. "Hey, buddy, how's it going?" *I'm dead below the waist; welcome to the graveyard.*

"It's going. Just finished cutting up that old man's chicken for him."

"Isn't that the sweetest?" I chirped like an elementary school teacher. *It is noble to aid our elders, dear sexless being with whom I'm civilly interacting.*

"Well, his arthritis is acting up and I'm a natural," he said, wiggling his non-arthritic fingers.

I patted him on the arm. "Aw, you are such a good egg."

Women use words like "buddy" and "good egg" to push men into the fiery lake of eternal friendship. Other terms women use include, but are not limited to: amigo, buddy, champ, bud, friend, dude, man, and bro. I was going to extinguish this thing the old-fashioned way: through subtle insinuation. He wouldn't know why it was happening, but he'd feel the distance slowly building. Maybe he'd attribute it to hormones dying down or his waning interest. Either way, he'd be none the wiser to the process.

"Florence, what are you doing?"

"Huh?" I sang sweetly.

"You sound like a lobotomized life coach. Since when have you ever called me buddy? That's what you call a dog."

"That's just how I talk." I shrugged. "Maybe you don't know me as well as you thought."

He looked at me with pursed lips, then suddenly grabbed my wrist and marched directly over to Officers Ramsey and Carmel. "I need to have a private word with Florence. We'll be right over there. Five minutes tops."

Officer Carmel stood and hiked up his pants intimidatingly. "That's not happening. Now why don't you give me your name, and tell me what interest you have in talking to my prisoner?"

Jonathan looked at Officer Ramsey, who was staring at his steaming coffee cup.

"Sit down and shut up, rookie."

"But he can't—"

"If you make me repeat myself, I'll put your ass in a sling."

Officer Carmel sat down with a harrumph, and Officer Ramsey continued to avoid Jonathan's eyes. "Five minutes."

Jonathan dragged me by the wrist to a corner stacked high with 1940s wooden highchairs. Faded Mickey Mouse cartoons smiled at me from the cushions. Naïve rat.

Jonathan released my wrist and leaned against the wood-paneled wall. "So what's wrong? Why are you acting weird?"

"Nothing's wrong, and I'm not acting weird. This is how I am. Maybe you never realized it."

"Oh, right, because *I don't know you at all.*" Jonathan stepped toward me, squinting his deep blue eyes. "I know you haven't always talked to me like a three-year-old."

I exhaled through my nose. "Listen, I just—I think we should take a step back. This Sexy Friendship isn't going to work."

"Why?"

"I . . . I thought I started to have feelings for you—only for a millisecond or two, but then I realized that was dumb and that I don't like you at all and that Sexy Friendship is too much because it can trick you into having feelings that you don't have. Because . . . like I said . . . I don't like you like that." The bold-faced lie felt like frostbite on my tongue. It was better, I reminded myself, than dealing with this thing falling apart organically. Nip it in the bud.

"Bull shit, Florence!" Jonathan snapped. "I know you want to be with me. Just admit that you're scared!"

"I'm not scared of you."

"Well, duh, I elicit a fear factor of negative ten. I'm like a bunny made out of marshmallows."

"A Peep?"

Jonathan was not entertained. "You're scared of being with someone who knows you—"

"Don't fucking analyze me." It was the first time I had sworn at Jonathan, but I was too livid to care. "You know what I'm scared of? Coming home and having the person I love say that I'm not enough for them, and finding out they've already found someone else. AGAIN."

Jonathan looked at me wide-eyed. "That's not going to happen!"

"I've heard that before," I insisted. "It won't matter if we're living together or we're married with kids; you'll eventually give in to your biological urge to spread your seed and run off with some girl named Tiff. You'll meet at Lowe's, she'll know how to fix a sink, and OH BOY, there is nothing sexier than that!"

"I can fix my own sink, I don't need a Tiff!"

"You say that now."

"What kind of rebuttal is that? I say that now, and I'll say it later. I don't want anyone but you. You are my Tiff."

"I'm not—"

"Yes, you are, but that's what you don't see!" he shouted. A few customers looked our way. He quieted down. "You are so busy being scared of another girl coming into the picture that you can't see what's right in front of you! I have never cheated—and will never cheat—on anyone! If we break up, it will be over a personality thing, a family thing, an ethics thing, or something else! Not another girl. When I date someone, I'm off-limits. I'm all in."

"Until some girl with Aphrodite's tits and a wind-chime laugh walks in."

"No! Not even then. You really don't trust me at all, do you?"

"It's not that! I just know human nature, and you're human."

"You're human too! Doesn't that mean you could walk out on me for another guy?"

"No, I would never do that!"

I bit my lip at the hypocrisy. I stood exposed, unable to speak. His eyes weren't accusing; they were sad—tired, even.

"If we are going to do this, you have to face your past, your demons, whatever you want to call it. Not for me, but for yourself. Because you can't be looking over your shoulder, waiting for the other shoe to drop. It's not fair to yourself."

I could hear the unspoken next sentence: *And it's not fair to me.*

He gave my elbow a light squeeze. "I have to get back."

CHAPTER 46

The Shrine

When I returned to my cell, I lay down on my bed, but I was too anxious to stay there for long. So I got up and brushed my teeth. Then I brushed them again. Then a third time, just for good measure. I was thorough. I mean, I really got in there. I even brushed the back of my tongue (the part everyone hates because you gag EVERY TIME). When I had no more enamel left to spare, I combed out my curls. I took my time untangling every knot. Once I finished, I put my fro in a bun and decided to do some sit-ups. That didn't last long. So I grabbed my new *National Geographic* and lay down again, but I couldn't focus.

I put my pillow over my face, trying to quash my thoughts, but it was useless. So I finally gave in.

I mentally washed my hands and feet like a devoted high priestess, and visited the moment as I had almost every night since its time. For years, I had kept it from judging eyes and clinical psychologists, but Jonathan had caught the scent of my burnt offerings. My mind retrieved it delicately.

His coffin disappeared into the earth's exposed core. My wrinkled wool skirt refused to lie flat against my tights. I hadn't picked it out. Holly had laid out my outfit the night before, and I had shuffled numbly to the dresser and put it on without looking in the mirror. Holly managed to put waterproof mascara on my right eye before I pulled away and sat in the car. No makeup was going to cover up the depression that weighed on me like an anchor.

After the funeral, through sobs that rendered our mutual friends unrecognizable, I saw Her. I saw Her with heart-wrenching clarity.

A deep sigh escaped Her red lips. Her blonde hair was in a tight bun, save for one strand flitting in the wind. Her heavy eyelashes bounced off high cheekbones, leaving black lines in their wake. Her slight frame shook with sorrow.

I could not look away.

Inconsolable pain colored Her narrow face. But there! There, in the raised corners of Her mouth, I saw it. A small comfort. A morbid, but altogether true, comfort that She fell back on in Her most private moments: he loved Her, and in his last moments, if he reflected on his life at all, Hers was the face that flashed before his eyes.

My three years of having part of him was nothing compared to her five months of having all of him. For that short time, he loved her completely.

And though I had wanted it with all my heart, I never had that with him.

She haunted me day and night, reminding me that no matter who I was with, there would always be a Woman, just like Her, who was more beautiful, more kind, and more desirable than I could ever be. For the rest of my life, I would be second best to Her.

I hated Her and longed to be Her. Wished Her ill and feigned to care nothing about Her. She was my obsession—and my curse.

But I had to let Her go. My ex was a passing season of both joy and pain. And She—she was the catalyst of that pain, not the cause. Hating her wasn't going to heal me. Nothing I could have done would've made him love her less and me more. She was his person. And once you've found that person, nothing will change your mind.

Which meant that if Jonathan was my person . . . no one could change his mind about me.

And with that thought, I lost it. Not an adorable, rosy-nosed, sniffling cry, but a hyperventilating, soul-cleansing, snot-lava eruption of tears—a pure, unadulterated Ugly Cry. I cried for the past, for the present, for the future I never had, for the future I faced, and for all I had lost. I burned down my shrine, my pillow so soaked in saltwater that I thought I would die of dehydration and heartbreak.

I didn't die, though. I survived the sadness and the pain.

I got up the next morning, drank a glass of water, and carried forth lighter than before.

CHAPTER 47

Patience

I spent the days leading up to the next Seminar pacing my cell. I paced for hours, oscillating between humility, bravery, shame, and nervousness. Was this how healthy people were supposed to handle anxiety? I felt like I was going to burst with emotions! This was why I preferred to repress them! But there was no turning back. I had to live this rollercoaster until I saw Jonathan again.

But when I went back to The Open Door, Jonathan was nowhere to be seen.

What in the frozen hell?! Did he understand the emotional gymnastics I went through to get here? He should've told me he was calling off!

. . . Then again, last week was a hot mess. It would've been natural for it to slip his mind. With grad school coming up, he probably had to buy books, register for classes, or something.

Blerg!

I guessed waiting another week wouldn't actually kill me.

CHAPTER 48

MIA

I was right. Waiting another week didn't kill me . . . but it came close. Nervous energy was exploding out of my every orifice. I explored Coffee's outdated library to see how long it took a person to die of dysentery, but the results were inconclusive. WebMD was more helpful: I either had Irritable Bowel Syndrome or all the cancers.

If I was dying, I could at least be comforted by knowing that my latest Decaf date could read me my last rites. He was a high priest of a peculiar cult, one whose members worshiped by computer light in their tissue-laden sanctuaries with their lubed-up hands and hunched frames. It was rare that such a pious man would emerge from his lair to interact with a real woman (they much prefer waxed women with silicon boobs), but this one was a curious little zealot. Unfortunately, his curiosity went unquenched; I was too distracted by Jonathan's absence to engage with him. Yup, Jonathan had called off two Fridays in a row.

Calling off one week, okay, but two? Something was up.

Every time the kitchen door swung open, I compulsively checked to see if he was there. I didn't know why, but it itched like a bug bite in the back of my mind. What if he was just keeping out of sight? Did he call off or was he avoiding me? Was I being paranoid or perceptive?

In order to put my fears to rest, on the way back from the restroom (with Lenny in slow pursuit), I walked up to the host. "Hi—Roy, right? I don't think we've officially met. I'm Florence."

"I know who you are. You're the one always distracting Jonathan and Bekah while I work my ass off."

"Um, yeah, that's me. Guess I didn't think about it that way. Sorry."

"Your apology is about six months too late," he snapped. "You know, I have a girlfriend, and I would love to hang out with her and fool around all the time, but I have a job to do, and I take it very seriously!"

I was going to interject, but it seemed like he'd needed to get this off his chest for a while.

"I work hard all night," he continued, "and it'd be nice to have my coworkers doing the same thing, not shooting the breeze with their friends! We have a tip pool, did you know that? If they slack, I lose money."

I waited, but he seemed to have tired himself out. "Roy, I'm sorry. That was inconsiderate of us. Speaking of the devil, though, I'm actually looking for Jonathan."

"Of course you are."

"Is he here?"

His piggish nose twitched. "Well, you haven't seen him around, have you?"

"No."

"Well then, I guess he's not here."

"All righty, Roy. Thanks for your help. I guess I'll see him next week."

But I didn't. Instead, I spent that evening with a man who will henceforth be referred to by his Native American name: Hands in Trench Coat.

It did not go well.

CHAPTER 49

The Latter Platter

I hated this. It had been a full month since I had seen Jonathan, and it was all I could think about. I was supposed to be a twenty-first-century woman, not a man-obsessed lemming, damn it! Of course, I was locked up, with nothing better to do than ruminate, so I guess it's understandable. A girl's gotta kill time somehow.

Excuses aside, I was drowning in suspense and regret. Why had I put off being honest with him for so long? Why didn't I put on my big-girl pants and tell him, "Hey, relationships scare me, let's figure it out together"? Why did I have to be a psycho about it?

Now, it was too late. If the Release Board approved me, I was getting out in six days, and I wouldn't have an excuse to go back to The Open Door.

"The artichoke dip here is awesome," my date, Carter, offered through my preoccupied haze. "If you're feeling it, we could split it."

Carter was nicely dressed, polite, and well-spoken—by all accounts a nice, average kid. But I was not deceived. The local Mormon boys were hitting that post-high school sweet spot, and this one was trying to make good with his Creator.

Whatever. I wasn't complaining; weathering a non-sexualized conversation with some spiritual prodding would be a pleasant distraction from the Jonathan conundrum.

Out of habit, I glanced toward the kitchen for Jonathan. In the middle of scolding myself for being such a pathetic stalker, I saw a familiar head of hair through the oval kitchen window. My stomach imploded. Jonathan was here. In the kitchen.

I tried to stay calm.

Slowly, I got up and walked over to the guard's table. "Lenny, mind if I go to the bathroom on my own?"

"All right, sweetheart, don't run out on me."

On the way, I stopped by Roy's podium again. "How's it going?"

"Fine," he replied stiffly.

"Is Jonathan around?" *Don't lie to me, you goblin.*

He ruffled his feathers. "He doesn't work here anymore, okay?" Before I could say another word, he flicked his wrist. "Move along."

CHAPTER 50

Maybe

Maybe I was wrong. Maybe it was a false sighting. Maybe there was a legitimate reason I hadn't seen Jonathan in weeks.

Maybe he was sick.

Or maybe he realized he was gay and felt guilty for leading me on, and that's why he was avoiding me.

Or maybe he was married, and his wife found out about me, and now he was forbidden to return to The Open Door.

Or maybe he got called away to an international business conference in the middle of nowhere Sierra Leone with no access to pen and paper, and I missed his smoke signals because of an unseasonal Nor'easter.

Or maybe he was a mafioso who cut a deal with the feds and was now in a witness protection program.

Or maybe he fell into a meat grinder and got turned into spicy sausage.

Or maybe he got in a car accident and woke up with retrograde amnesia.

Or maybe he was practicing walking on stilts when a helicopter decapitated him.

Or maybe he had an aneurism.

Or maybe he was walking past a fireplace, and the dry-cleaning agent on his pants caught fire, and he was incinerated.

Or maybe he went to Jurassic Park and got eaten by a raptor.

. . . Or maybe I had pushed him away one too many times, and ruined everything.

CHAPTER 51

Compassion in a Box

"Hey, I meant to ask, how was your Seminar?" Susie the Strangler asked. "Did Jonathan finally show up?"

Any composure I had gathered to do chores was lost with that question. I let out a sob and, in an effort not to make a scene, grabbed a dirty pillowcase and cried into it. The pillowcase smelled like a boar puked up sauerkraut on a stray cat. Of course I had grabbed Gretchen's pillowcase. This. This was my life.

"Darlin', what's wrong?" Susie the Strangler asked.

I grabbed a different pillowcase and wiped my eyes. Thankfully, no one else in the room seemed to notice my breakdown. Nympho Yvette was captivating everyone with one of her coming-of-age sagas. "And then my gynecologist lost his artificial hand during the exam!"

"Jonathan's over it," I managed to say.

"Over what?"

I waved my hand around my head. "All of this. Me."

"Did he say that? Was he there last night?"

"I saw him in the kitchen. That's where he's been hiding."

She sighed. "I was hoping he quit or got fired."

"Nope, just evasive as hell."

"Maybe he has mono or something?"

I shook my head. It was a nice thought, but no, he wasn't sick. He was sick of dealing with me.

"I hate this!" I said. "Is this what love is?! Putting your heart on the line even though nine times out of ten, you get screwed over?"

"Yep."

"Why do we do it?" I asked, exasperated.

She shrugged. "We want someone to light our birthday candles."

I started to cry again.

She threw her arm around me and rested her head on my shoulder. "That a girl. Let it out."

"I miss the days when I could hold it together." I blew my nose into the pillowcase and threw it in the washer.

"You're movin' in the right direction. Better this than feelin' nothin' at all."

"If you say so."

Later that evening, I heard a light tapping on my cell bars. I lifted my head up from my pillow and saw Greg standing outside the door. I wasn't really up for talking, but I couldn't pretend I didn't see him. I got up, my head groggy from all the emotions of the day.

"Hey."

He gave me a small smile. "Hey, how are you?"

"I'm okay, you?"

"I was in the laundry room today."

"Oh."

"Yeah, I overheard."

"Ah."

"So how are you, actually?"

As much as I didn't want to talk about it, there was a part of me that needed my friend. "You called it. Jonathan didn't know me, and when he got to know me, he dropped me. Sooo . . . yeah, you were right."

"I was afraid of that." He reached through the cell bars, squeezed my wrist, and released it. We stood quiet for a few seconds before Greg furrowed his brow. "You know what, screw that guy! If he's not smart enough to know how awesome you are, then he doesn't deserve you."

"Please. I'm damaged goods. All I'm bringing to the table is a criminal record and a bunch of prison stories that aren't party-appropriate. He's funny and great, and he's finally figured out that he can have whoever he wants. I'm the bottom of the barrel."

The lights in the hallway were dimmed, but I could see Greg shaking his head emphatically. "You are not the bottom of the barrel. You are the top of the barrel. You are outside the barrel. That's how great you are. He's the one with the problem. He's scum. He's the scum that forms in between scum's toes. You are too good for scum."

I smiled. "Thanks for saying that."

"I'm just telling the truth."

"Well, thanks."

"Um, so . . . I was going to wait to give this to you." He pulled out something the size of a shoebox from behind his back. "It was supposed to be your getting-out gift."

I reached out and took the gift. It was a vintage silver jewelry box covered in tiny square mirrors.

"I found it at an antique store. It reminded me of your grandma's. The one you said that you played dress up with."

"Wow, I don't even remember telling you about that." Warm tears streamed down my face. I licked my lips, tasting the salty mix of joy and sorrow. "Thank you."

He looked at his feet. "I'm sorry it's not wrapped. I was going to wrap it before I gave it to you, but, I don't know, I figured you could use it now. Hopefully, it makes you feel a little better."

His childlike vulnerability panged my insides. Up until now, I had been planning on ending our friendship; meanwhile, he'd been searching for a jewelry box from a half-remembered conversation. How could I be so willing to discard his friendship, even under the guise of sparing him? Wasn't he worth fighting for? He was there when the rest of the world preferred to forget about me. Wasn't that the kind of person I wanted, even needed, around?

"Thank you," I repeated, hugging him through the bars. I could feel his fuzzy curls stick to my tear-spattered cheeks.

He squeezed tightly. "Love you, Flo."

CHAPTER 52

Baggage Check

After everyone had gone to bed, I pulled the jewelry box from under my pillow, turning it in my hands. The tarnished mirrors reflected my grandmother's eyes; I smiled at the memory.

She and I were playing dress up with her good jewelry. Who knows why she let me touch it. Like all kids, I was needlessly destructive and clumsy so, inevitably, while she was in the kitchen, I broke the latch on one of her bracelets. To my horror, I couldn't fix it with my sticky fingers, so I hid in the closet. When she returned, she found me nestled between the winter coats.

Scooping me up in her arms, the way she'd done with my mother before me, she exclaimed, "I thought I lost you! Why are you hiding?"

Between sobs, I confessed.

"Look at me," she demanded, holding my guilt-ridden frame in her arms. "Florence, look at Grandma." I lifted my head tentatively, meeting her familiar brown eyes. "Even if you broke all my jewelry, I would still love you. No if, ands, or buts. I love you no matter what."

For a minute there, Jonathan had me convinced that he was also blind to my transgressions. Perhaps he believed it himself until we fought, and he woke up the next day thinking, *What the hell am I doing? I need this baggage like a pumice enema. I'm going to find myself a nice, uncomplicated girl.*

My heart lurched at the thought. I knew this was going to happen. This was what always happened when you opened yourself up!

For a moment, I was tempted to dive into the abyss, the one where I suffocated on despair and hopelessness while simultaneously dissecting my insecurities. I'd done it before, and (*tosses glitter over head*) with finesse! But being martyred is too easy.

It's too easy to assume that when something doesn't work out, nothing will. The harder truth is that not everything pans out. Life is a constant balance of celebrations and lamentations—a mixed bag of innocent prisoners and corrupt wardens, laughter and milk-spewing noses, loose teeth and lost children, loyal spouses and cheating exes. To accept one and reject the other is madness. But to accept them all is a wrestling match that'll earn you a name.

Jonathan was a blessing: a reminder that my heart was capable of more than murmuring. But for better or worse, it was over. Maybe someday, I would end up with someone like my grandma or Greg—someone who would love me, even in my brokenness.

Because as fun as Sexy Friendship was, in the end, it wasn't real life. Yes, real life is flirting, holidays, and inside jokes. But it is also complicated situations, bad moods, and long days (and weeks and months). No one can be the best version of themselves all the time, and I was no exception.

If things needed to be all rainbows and butterflies for Jonathan to stick around, it was better that he bailed now. Because goodness forbid we dated, went through an extended honeymoon period, and got married. If I thought this was hard, getting divorced would've been unbearable.

Small mercies.

CHAPTER 53

Worry and Angst: Two Peas in a Pod

For the next five days, thoughts of Jonathan were replaced with anxiety about the Release Board's decision. I had taken it for granted that my Decaf dates gave me positive reviews. The more I thought about it, the more I was convinced that I'd screwed the pooch.

First off, I had called out Vincent for being a deadbeat father. What was I thinking? There are tons of shitty parents in this world, and I had to call out *that one*?

Then, I got in a bickering match with Kev. I thought it was all in good fun, and that his evaluation would reflect that, but what if he said I was disrespectful? What if he told them that I likened his package to a baby carrot? For the love of Pete, why couldn't I just keep my big mouth shut???

And what about my other dates? What if I was too distracted by Jonathan and they stated that I was aloof and antisocial? What if they felt neglected, and they complained about it on their evaluations?

The reality was, I didn't know what they'd been thinking when the pen hit the paper. They could've drawn me with devil horns and a spiked tail for all I knew.

I felt sick.

If I screwed this up, I'd never forgive myself. And I'd have a lifetime to think about it.

CHAPTER 54

You Don't Have to Go Home, but You Can't Stay Here

Finally, on June 14, it was time for the Release Board to make their decision.

When the conference room doors shut, I tried to tell myself that there was nothing to worry about. *I can't have been the worst they've ever seen. Hell, look at Gretchen! All in all, I'm an adequate prisoner with a clean record.*

But the self-talk didn't lessen the terror.

I was terrified that I would never again go for a bike ride. Terrified that I would never again see the summit of a mountain or a coral reef. Terrified that I'd never again dress in normal clothes or go to a hockey game. Most of all, I was terrified that Jonathan backing out was a sign from God that I shouldn't get attached to anyone, because I was in for the long haul.

Two hours of cold sweats later, the board members emerged with their decision: we were all fit for human consumption.

Ecstasy coursed through the whole Coffee Pot. There was dancing, hugging, laughing, making calls to family members, and dreaming of solo showers and freedom. The Domestics compiled a recipe book for us, First Lady Abigail and Yosemite

Karen sang us a duet, and Gretchen, wrought with emotion, bid us good fortune with a twenty-one-burp salute. Dr. Sean even threw us a little Decaf party to celebrate, complete with cupcakes, take-home stress balls, and an ill-fated game of Truth or Dare. Say what you want about shrinks, they throw kick-ass parties.

Greg stopped by to offer his congratulations. "I wish I could be here to see you off tomorrow, but I have to drop my mom off at the airport."

"Via bus?"

He shrugged. "She likes my company."

I smiled. It was the first positive thing I'd heard him say about anyone in his family. "Okay, well, where do you want to eat this weekend? My dad never got the grill to work, so we're going out."

He touched his head to mine. "I want to go wherever you want."

"All right," I said, backing up. "I'll let you know."

"You know I'll be there."

I nodded, breaking the prolonged eye contact by stuffing a cupcake in my mouth.

When he left, Susie the Strangler approached me. "Is there something going on between you guys?"

"I uhn-oh." I shrugged.

"Woman, finish that cupcake. We are having this conversation."

"In 'at case . . ." I grabbed another cupcake and shoved it in my mouth.

At last, we said our final goodbyes to the ones we were leaving behind. It was more difficult than I'd anticipated. Somewhere along the way, I had grown to love this ragtag group of women with their funny quirks and surprising humanity. Though flawed and scarred, they were beautiful, with rich lives, unexpected gifts, and open hearts. An outsider would never be able to appreciate all they had to offer—and for a breath, I was grateful to be an insider.

CHAPTER 55

Freedom

I spent my first half hour of freedom sitting on the curb, waiting for my parents to pick me up in their new car. I had forgotten how little Coffee looked like a prison from the front. When I got bussed in five years ago, I remembered thinking it looked like an inner-city middle school. There was no barbed wire fence, no watchtowers—only a long, brick building with a greenhouse on the east wing.[34]

The early summer wind gusted against my face, but sweat still poured down my cheeks onto my upper lip. I had transferred to Coffee in the middle of winter, so my "release outfit" was a wool sweater and jeans. Not only was it hot, it was snug. After all the years of subpar meals, I'd figured that I would be swimming in my old clothes, but no—it seemed the prison diet was no diet at all. But I'd rather be hot and chubby out here than cool and thin behind bars.

The air that filled my lungs was the same air in the courtyard, but it tasted different. It was fresher, almost sweet. Every

---

34 Maybe they figured that being out in the middle of nowhere was protection enough from runaways, so they only barbwired the courtyard. Or maybe they were too cheap to splurge on the extra fence.

molecule in my body was stretching its legs.[35] I wanted to run, skip, roll around in the dirt, and rediscover every feeling I had missed in the last five years.

So I started with jumping into my parents' arms, my tears mixing with theirs as we celebrated the end of the long journey we took on two different sides of Coffee's cinderblock walls.

---

35 Yes, molecules have legs in this metaphor. Don't be difficult.

CHAPTER 56
Life on the Outside

"SIT!" Greg yelled. "SIIIIIIT!"

My puppy, Harper, turned his head from side to side, his big ol' Bassett Hound ears swinging. He wagged his tail, but stayed standing.

Evening had fallen outside my parents' small brick house, where I'd been staying since my release. With its shag rugs, outdated wood paneling, and shelves of Memorable Moment figurines, it hadn't changed since my childhood. My parents had carpooled to bingo, leaving Greg and me to train Harper.

"You've clearly never trained a dog before. You have to do this." I held Harper's little furry chest and pushed his butt down. "Sit. See? He'll begin to associate sitting with the word now."

"All right, Dog Whisperer. But I still give the best belly rubs! Oh don't I, Harper?" Greg rolled Harper over and started rubbing his belly.

Harper's tongue fell out the side of his mouth in pure bliss.

Greg looked up at me with his soft brown eyes and childlike smile. "Hey, what do you say about me taking you and Harper out for ice cream? Then we can drop him off back here and go to a movie?"

It had been a month since I got out of Coffee, and life was moving forward. I'd gotten Harper and started my job, my parents had fully recovered from their surgeries, and Greg had actually gotten his license. I was, more or less, establishing a "new normal." I had every reason to be happy with my life, but Jonathan still hung over my head like a broken halo. Even though Greg had proved himself to be a good, loyal guy, Jonathan still lingered in the back of my mind. I was going to fix it, but until then I couldn't say yes to any sort of date with Greg without feeling dishonest, so I dodged it.

"Can we rain-check?"

"Sure. Do you just want to stay here and watch something?"

"Actually, I have to go somewhere," I said, getting up.

"Where?"

"I have a dentist appointment." I was such a bad liar. It was seven at night. What kind of nocturnal dentist was I seeing?

"Oh." He gave me a bemused smile. "Want me to go with you?"

"I'm gunna go solo this time, but let's do something tomorrow, okay?"

"Sure. Mind if I play with Harper a little longer?"

"No problem. Just lock up when you leave."

Forty-five minutes later, I stood in front of The Open Door, clenching a letter made translucent from my hand sweat.

I heaved a breath and stepped through the door. A familiar voice squealed from across the room. "FLORENCE!"

I smiled back half-heartedly. "Oh, hey, Bekah. Welcome back."

"Thanks! Spain was amazing!" She glowed in her naïve-college-girl way. "I ate dinner at ten every night, had the best sangria ever, and the soccer was insane! But look at you! You're out! How are you?" She looked at me sympathetically. "I'm sorry about the Jonathan thing."

She was across the ocean and she knew before I did. GREAT.

I handed her the letter. "Can you give this to him?"

"Um, okay? What does it say?"

All the hustle and bustle of the restaurant stopped, holding its breath for my answer.

"It says that I won't see him anymore." With gracious determination, I added, "No hard feelings."

Bekah took the envelope silently, then looked up at me with red-hot fire in her eyes. "Are you fucking kidding?"

"What?"

"He really, really liked you and now that he needs you, you ditch him? What is wrong with you? Give it to him yourself, you selfish bitch!" She shoved the letter against my chest.

"What the hell are you talking about?" I yelled back. "He avoided me for weeks, and I'm trying to be the bigger person here, so CRAWL OUT OF MY ASS and give him the damn letter!" I pushed it into her hands.

Bekah examined me, her furrowed eyebrows rising slightly. "You don't know."

"Know what?" I asked.

"No one told you. I mean, who would? I've been gone; Roy hates you, no offense, and no one else really knows. Still, someone should have told—"

"Bekah! What don't I know?"

"Jonathan's been in a coma at Acadia Hospital for two months. He—"

"N-no," I stuttered. "I saw him in the kitchen."

"No, you didn't. He hasn't been here."

"Yes, I did," I said through gritted teeth. Taking the high road was hard enough without her giving me a hard time. I just wanted to go home and move on with my life. "He was here. I know he was here."

"You're crazy!" she bellowed. "He is in the hospital!"

"I'm not crazy!" I shouted back. "I SAW HIM!"

"Not unless he was SLEEP WALKING during his COMA."

"He was in the kitchen," I said stubbornly.

"Oh my God." Bekah seized my arm and yanked me through the kitchen door. "He's not here. I don't know how to make it any clearer!"

I looked around: giant dishwasher, stainless steel counter with colorful plated food, and the back of Jonathan's head. I opened my mouth, ready to point out that maybe Bekah was the one losing it, when he turned toward me. And unless Jonathan had gotten plastic surgery, it wasn't him.

"He's in the hospital," I said, finally starting to compre-hend it. "In a coma. He's not here."

"That's what I've been trying to tell you!" Bekah said, with a sigh of relief.

"I have to go."

She took off her nametag. "I'll go with you."

"No, it's okay," I said quickly. "I'll go alone."

CHAPTER 57

Complications

In the ten minutes it took me to get from The Open Door to Acadia Hospital, my mind raced. I had rushed off before Bekah could tell me what happened, and my worry was next level. Was it a car accident? A shoot-out? Did he slip in the shower? Was he paralyzed? Would he ever wake up? What if I didn't get there in time and he passed away?

I dashed into the hospital lobby, feigned charity by pushing a wheelchair-bound slowpoke out of my way, and stopped, light-headed, at the reception desk.

"Jonathan," I panted. "Diaz."

The heavily spray-tanned woman behind the counter didn't look up from her phone. "You family? Family visitation only."

"I'm his sister." The lie slipped out like a water birth. "I just got into town. I NEED TO SEE HIM. Please! Right now!"

"Okay, okay, give me a second." She raised her painted-on eyebrows. "G42. The elevator is down the hall. Go to the second floor, turn left, and you'll be in G. Even numbers are on the right."

I sprinted through the hospital labyrinth until I stood huffing and puffing in front of G42. I went to fix my hair, but then I remembered, *oh yeah, coma*.

Cautiously, I walked in. A young woman in maroon jeans and a gray sweatshirt sat beside the bed, crying into a crumbled tissue. His sister Jenn—it had to be; she was just as he had described, with long, dark brown hair and a dark complexion. She looked up at me with her puffy blue eyes and sniffled. "They're doing emergency surgery right now."

My throat constricted in terror. "Oh no."

"It's going to be okay, it has to be." She attempted to compose herself. "I'm sorry, who are . . ."

She trailed off and stared at me for a few seconds. "It's you. You came. I didn't think . . ." Her lip trembled, and tears trickled down her cheeks. "I'm sorry, I'm usually not this overcome. It's just . . . there was so much blood." She buried her face in her hands.

"What happened?"

"There was a complication with the vaginoplasty."

"Wait, I'm sorry . . . a complication with what?"

"Yeah," she said, "that's the technical term for it. Don't worry, I didn't know before either. 'Sex change' rolls off the tongue easier."

The rest of her words wouldn't compute. Smoldering hot brain leaked out my ears and down my neck.

I had mentally prepared for every scenario: legs amputated, hands scalded, nose gone, but I had not, even in my most paranoid moments, prepared for the truth that was staring me in the face. That Jonathan Diaz—The Open Door waiter, covert Mexican, and front-runner in the race to be the father of my children—just got a big-ass sex change.

CHAPTER 58

Diana

"So, it's . . . it's . . . it's official?" That was all I could muster while trying to reconcile "Jonathan" and "sexual reassignment surgery."

"Yes!" she said, smiling through her tears. "I don't know if she ever told you, but I was the first one who knew she was a woman on the inside. I caught her trying on my prom dress. I was so ticked off." She laughed. "Didn't want her giant shoulders to break the straps. I couldn't have cared less about the gender thing."

I nodded blankly. "What is . . . *her* new name now?"

"She didn't tell you? That's so like her. She loves surprises."

"She loves surprises," I echoed.

"Her name is Diana. She thought it fit." Jenn bit her lip. "You know, she told me about you. About the fight you had."

"He . . . she did?"

"Yes."

I shook my head. "I pushed him . . . um, I mean her, away. I was afraid of a relationship. I'm not good with emotions. And love things in general."

"She was afraid, too—afraid that you wouldn't accept the surgery."

I didn't know what to say. I wasn't transphobic, but I also wasn't a lesbian (or even an alcohol-induced bisexual), so the idea of kissing *Diana* didn't appeal to me at all. Even knowing that it was still Jonathan on the inside . . . it wouldn't negate the fact that he was physically a woman. Maybe he was right to assume I wouldn't "accept" the surgery. What kind of person did that make me?

"You changed things for her, you know," Jenn continued. "For years, she was too afraid to be herself, but when she met you, she felt like things finally fell into place. But she never told me your name."

"My name's Florence."

"It's nice to meet you, Florence."

"You too."

She took my hand. "Listen, I know you preferred her the way she was, but this is for the best. And the fact you are here . . . it shows that you really care for her."

"I do. But it's complicated. I—"

"It's a lot to take in, I know." She squeezed my hand. "But you two will work through this. In the grand scheme of things, this is just a bump in the road."

Helplessly, I squeezed her hand in return. "It's just . . . Jonathan didn't tell me about *any* of this."

"Who's Jonathan?"

"I mean Diana." I couldn't believe I was having this conversation. "I only knew her as a male, as Jonathan."

"Jonathan?" She furrowed her brow. "Her name was Dave."

"Dave? Her name was Dave before the surgery?"

"Yeah?"

"I thought his name was Jonathan."

"No, it was Dave. Always has been."

"Well, he told his coworkers and me that his name was Jonathan. Are you saying that he lied to us?" Lying about a life-changing surgery, I get, but lying about something as simple as his name? Was everything he told me a lie?

"I don't know," she said, "but I've never heard of a Jonathan. What's going on?"

"You tell me!" I shouted. "Because apparently, your brother Dave who is now your sister Diana told me his/her name was Jonathan and I don't know what the hell is happening!"

She looked befuddled. "Hon, I think you're in the wrong room."

"No, this is room G42. Jonathan Diaz's room."

"This is G42a. There's a G42b next door."

"Are you sure?" I asked.

She blew her nose. "Pretty sure."

"Ah, well then," I said awkwardly, making my way to the door. "I better get going then. Uh, best wishes to you and Diana."

CHAPTER 59

Confessions

In Room G42b, the hospital bed closest to the window was empty, neatly made and ready for its next occupant. The other bed held Jonathan. His eyes were shut. Beside him, a heart monitor beeped steady and monotonous.

Hesitantly, I made my way to the bed and sank into the beige chair next to his shoulder.

My breath caught in my throat. It looked like Sweeney Todd had taken a razor to the left side of his face. There were three intersecting slash marks spanning from his eyebrow to his chin. They were healing, raised and pink now, but I could see the pockmarks where they'd removed the stitches.

With trembling fingers, I brushed his hair out of his deep-set eyes. "Jonathan?"

I had almost expected him to wake, flash a half-cocked smile, and tell me this was all an elaborate hoax, but his breathing remained steady, his pulse unchanged, his eyes closed.

Gingerly, I took his hand and pressed his knuckles to my lips. I breathed him in, his naturally woodsy scent masked by antiseptic.

"What happened to you?"

Again, he didn't answer.

Tears pooled in my eyes. I tried to blink them away, but they flooded down my cheeks. "Jonathan, I am so sorry. For everything. You were right. I was scared of getting hurt, and I pushed you away." I took a deep breath. "I'm out of Coffee now—a lot of things have changed since I last saw you. But the one thing that hasn't changed, even when I tried to change it, is how I feel about you. I, um . . . I—"

"OH PLEASE," a voice boomed from behind me. "Professing your love to a guy in a coma is *so* cliché, Flo."

I jumped, and turned to see Greg leering disapprovingly in the doorway, hands in his pockets.

"Greg, what are you doing here?"

"What are *you* doing here, Flo? What happened to your dentist appointment?"

I didn't know what to say. He had caught me red-handed. So I told him the truth. "I needed closure."

"Did you get it?" Greg walked around Jonathan's bed and sat on the other side. "Is this what you needed to feel better about things? Now you can move on?"

"Greg, I—I love him."

"How?! Look at him. He's a vegetable!"

"Don't say that."

"It's the truth, Flo. His brain is obviously a mashed potato now. You think he's going to be able to take you on dates or have a conversation? No! He's going to lie there, and every day it's going to be you and him in a hospital room."

"You don't know that."

He looked at the ceiling, rubbing his hands over his face. "I can't believe I'm competing with a vegetable and I'm losing."

"Stop calling him that!"

"Wake up, Flo! He's not going to come out of this and be totally fine. He's going to be like this for the rest of his life, however long that lasts. It's time you admit that it's over, and move on. With me. This guy was charming for a few months, but I have proven myself year after year. You know who I am, and you would be happy with me!"

"I'm sorry. I'm sorry that I've led you on. I—"

"Don't." He got up to leave the room, but stopped at the doorway. He didn't look at me, just started into the hall. "Just tell me. Did I ever stand a chance?"

I bit my lip. I had been asking myself the same question. Asking it was hard enough, but knowing the answer was excruciating. "Greg, I'm sorry."

He didn't move. Still staring out into the hallway.

"Greg?"

He didn't answer.

"Greg, I'm sorry. I'm so sorry. I never meant for this—"

He slammed the hospital room door shut and pulled out a knife. "No, Flo, I'm sorry."

My blood curdled.

"I'm sorry it had to come to this. I've tried. I've really, really tried." He laughed, but there was no humor in his voice. "Do you know how long I have loved you?"

"Greg. Please—"

"NO! YOU ANSWER ME. HOW LONG DO YOU THINK I'VE LOVED YOU?"

I stared at the knife trembling in his hand. "Five . . . five years."

"Wrong." His lip curled upward in a sneer. "Seven years. I have loved you for seven years."

I shook my head.

"Don't believe me?" He waved the knife around like an orchestra conductor. "Seven years ago on October twenty-third, I saw you at the farmer's market wearing your matching hat and gloves—you know, the ones with the dancing reindeer on them."

He smiled at the knife. "You were the most beautiful thing I'd ever seen. You were biting your soft pink lips, lost in thought, looking for the perfect apples. I knew from that day forward, my life would never be the same. My every breath, every thought, every dream was going to be about you. I knew I had to be with you."

His brow furrowed. "But you were with that pretentious jerk! I don't know what you saw in him. He didn't worship you! He didn't love you! He left you! For that pita-loving vegan whore, no less! It was like spitting in God's face!" He shook his head. "He hurt you. I couldn't stand to see you in pain. That's why I had to do it. It was the right thing to do."

My heart shrank. "What did you do?"

"Baby, I went to his house to tell him that someone so dumb didn't deserve to live . . . I did it for you!" His eyes were unblinking and manic. "I even used the scarf you didn't wear anymore so you wouldn't be upset! And yes, I felt guilty when you got arrested, but then I realized it was perfect! "You didn't have a record or any drug problems so I was able to pull some strings, and get you sentenced to Coffee!" He smiled widely. "It was fate. You were meant to be with me!"

I stared at that vicious smile. How had I never seen the instability—the obsession—behind it? Just a few hours ago, he had been smiling, rubbing Harper's belly. That boyish smile had transformed into something terrifying and unrecognizable.

"You . . . you killed him?" It didn't sound real, but as I repeated it, it sank in. "You *killed* him. You killed him and you stalked me!"

"Stalked is such an ugly word."

"You've always known too much about me!" I remembered that night when Greg listed all the things that Jonathan didn't know about me. I hadn't paid much attention to it then, but . . . my lost diploma, my hatred of bowling, my love of pigs, my crocheting with my mother—these were things I'd never shared with him or anyone else at Coffee. My mind raced, grasping at the memories. "My grandmother's jewelry box! You knew! You knew about it! I never told you about that, did I?!"

"You would have eventually," he said nonchalantly. "I'm not much of a gift-giver, but I thought, hey, it's a special occasion."

"How did you know about it? Have you been following me my whole life?" I asked in horror.

"Ha, no, Flo. Don't be ridiculous. I read it in your diary. You should find a different hiding place, by the way, because the whole under-the-mattress thing is overplayed." He examined my face. "Don't look at me like that. It all worked out in the end. You came to Coffee, and you fell in love with me. I won't apologize for that."

"I don't love you."

"No," he warned, pointing the knife at me, "you love me. A deep love that made you believe in yourself again."

"I hate you," I whispered.

"You don't need to lie to me, Flo! I know you better than that. What I don't know—what I can't wrap my head around—is how you could betray me for this guy! A . . . a . . . a . . . a . . . pussy!" He lit up at his word choice. "Yeah! He was a pussy! A big pussy! You should have seen him when he found me in his apartment. He screamed like a little girl and grabbed a pot off the stove. A pussy's weapon! Ha! You should've heard when I cut his face—he cried like the pussy he is! He shut up once I slammed his head into the coffee table."

"*You* did this?"

"It was an honest mistake," he said apologetically. "I meant to kill him, but his pussy screaming woke up the neighbor who started pounding on the door, saying he called the police. I had to sneak out the window." He chuckled. "You should've seen it: my pants got caught on a nail, and I almost had to ditch them. Can you imagine me running away in my boxers?"

"You are sick," I said. "You are psychotic! How did I not see it before?"

Greg walked up to me, his warm breath against my forehead. He slowly ran the edge of the knife along my jaw. "We see what we want to see, don't we? Now, move. I'm going to put the poor dog out of its misery."

"I'm not going anywhere." My knees felt like jelly, but I held my ground. He had hurt Jonathan once; he wasn't going to do it again.

"Move, Flo. I don't want to hurt you, but if you get in my way, you'll leave me no choice."

"You're going to kill a man in his sleep? You're a coward," I growled. "A fucking coward."

"Flo." He chuckled, tapping the tip of the knife against my breastbone. "That potty mouth of yours is going to get you in trouble someday."

"So you're not a coward?"

"No."

"Then kiss me."

He wobbled back. "What?"

"You heard what I said. Kiss me." I held his gaze. "You say you aren't a coward. Prove it."

"Do you think I'm stupid?"

"No, I think you keep making up excuses not to kiss me. You've had seven years, Greg. Do you want me or not?"

After a moment of hesitation, a breath caught before the dive, he went for it. And I—I took one for the team.

His gross rough tongue ran along my teeth and filled my mouth like a slimy bullfrog. I tore his shirt open and felt a slim-fitting wife beater hugging his twiggy frame. I yanked the button-up off his right shoulder, then his left. It crumpled to the floor. I pulled the wife beater over his head, leading him across the room, pushing him onto the empty hospital bed. He was breathing heavily, barely even able to open his crossed eyes as I straddled him.

"Run your fingers through my hair," I panted. With a clang, the knife fell to the ground, and he pushed his ten greedy fingers through my frizzy locks.

That was it. That was as far as I'd gotten in my plan. My strategy from there was vague at best: Keep him away from Jonathan. Keep him away from the knife.

I weighed my options as Greg sloppily bit my earlobe. I could make out with him until someone came in. But that was risky; what if no one came? His weird tiny lips made their way to my collarbone. *Ugh, okay, think, think, think, think.* I could choke him out. No, gravity wasn't on my side; he was stronger than me, he'd throw me off. His staggered breath was almost at my sternum. I needed to brainstorm faster, or else I was going to have to do this thing, and there wasn't enough bleach in the world to make that okay.

So with a passionate tumble, I rolled off the bed.

Greg stretched out his arm. "Flo!"

I scanned under the bed for the knife, but it wasn't there. Where the fuck did it go? Then I saw it. The four-inch metallic blade had slid almost under Jonathan's bed. I tried to propel myself across the floor, but it was a lot stickier than I anticipated[36], and I stopped short. I army crawled to the knife, my fingertips an inch away from the hilt when Greg, still half on the bed, grabbed my ankles and yanked me back.

He jumped off the bed and picked the knife. "I knew it, you lying bitch! What were you going to do? Kill me?"

Trembling, I stood up.

"Look at you, even the thought of killing a man is making you shake like a leaf," he said with pseudo-compassion. "But I can help with that."

With lightning-fast speed, he grabbed my right hand, then my left, squeezing them around the hilt of the knife. He dragged me over to Jonathan's bed. "We're going to do this together, babe."

"NO!" I screamed.

With his hands over mine, he brought the knife over my head. Time slowed. I could picture the trajectory of the knife: over my head, past my face, down into Jonathan's still-beating heart. Greg was too strong; there was nothing I could do to counter his strength. But if there was anything that I'd learned about life, it was that you could, with the smallest shift of direction, change the outcome.

And with that, I turned my wrists as hard as I could, and with Greg's strength behind me, plunged the knife into my stomach.

---

36 IT WAS *STICKY*. WHAT ARE WE EVEN PAYING YOU FOR, CDC?

Greg's hands left the knife as my knees buckled.

"Florence!" He knelt beside me, eyes wide with panic. "Are you okay?"

No, dipshit, I just stabbed myself. Was what I wanted to say, but for a moment it didn't hurt at all. Then I saw the blood trickling out along the sides of the knife. That's when the pain hit me. I had never experienced anything like it. It was excruciating. It throbbed like . . . like . . . well, I don't know! I've got no colorful analogy for you! IT HURT LIKE A MOTHER, OKAY??

"Help me," I moaned.

And, in an effort to help, Greg yanked the knife out.

I screamed as my blood spattered across his face. Greg turned white and froze—like a terrified ice sculpture.

I could feel the blood leaving my body with every heartbeat. This was *Saving Private Ryan* shit. I tried to put pressure on the wound, but my quivering hands got slippery with blood in seconds. The agonizing pain mixed with the smell of exsanguinating copper was too much. I vomited.

"GET A DOCTOR! A NURSE! SOMETHING!"

"Towels." Greg unfroze and darted to the bathroom. "I'll get towels! I'm going to get you towels! You'll be okay! Just listen to my voice! You'll be okay!"

My eyes watered, and darkness edged around the perimeter of my vision. Greg disappeared into the bathroom.

I heard a loud crash.

And in my last moments of consciousness, I could just make out a pair of stilettos clicking out of the bathroom over Greg's limp body.

CHAPTER 60

RIP

Then the darkness closed in, and I died.

CHAPTER 61

LOL

Just kiddingggggg.
　　Can you imagine?
　　Nah, read on, you crazy kid.

CHAPTER 62

Love Loss and Blood Loss

I opened my eyes.

Florescent lights. White ceiling. White walls.

I felt dizzy.

There was a throbbing in my stomach.

Where was I?

It didn't look like Coffee's infirmary. It was too big, too clean, too state-of-the-art. I turned my head. Dr. Sean sat next to the bed, clenching and unclenching his jaw. I went to sit up, but he stopped me. "You're going to rip your stitches."

I lay back down.

"Here." He took the hand control for my hospital bed and sat me up slowly. "Better?"

My head pounded. "Where am I?"

"Acadia Hospital. You sustained a serious abdominal injury, lost a lot of blood."

I pulled my hospital gown up from under the sheets. He wasn't kidding. There was a swollen, red, half-inch gash stitched across my gut. It looked like a miniature back-alley C-section. "What happened to me?"

Then it came back to me like a boomerang. "Greg! It was Greg! Dr. Sean, it was Greg!" I tried to scramble out of bed. "He killed my ex! He tried to kill Jonathan!"

"Florence, stop." He gently put his hand on my shoulder. "He's in custody. It's okay."

"What about Jonathan?" I asked woozily.

"He's fine; still comatose, but unharmed."

"Okay," I said, bracing myself against an invisible wave. Pain meds made me sick. Maybe this whole thing was a bad morphine trip. I lay back down.

"You're probably wondering why I'm here," Dr. Sean said.

"Not really," I replied honestly. "Considering what just happened, the presence of a mental health professional isn't a mystery."

Dr. Sean took a sharp breath. "I'm here unofficially. Or rather, off the record. The Warden could fire me if he knew I was here speaking to you, because what I'm about to tell you may give you grounds to sue Coffee. But I think you deserve to know."

"What?" I said apprehensively.

He paused. "Greg was on the Rehabilitation Board."

"Wh—"

"The year that you were admitted to Coffee, the Warden appointed him to the Board. He thought Greg could observe you all in a way that we couldn't. Greg was instructed to keep his ear to the ground and to report anything that slipped the Board's radar. Consequently, he reported antisocial behaviors that you were supposedly exhibiting and repeatedly argued that you were unfit to be enrolled in the Decaf Seminars. Until this year."

"How could you believe him?!" I yelled, sitting up in fury, stitches completely forgotten. "You're supposed to be able to tell when people are lying to you!"

"I had concerns with Greg's credibility early on. But when I brought it up to the Warden, he sided with Greg. That didn't stop me from advocating for you, as fruitless as it was."

"Yeah, right," I spat. "Why would the Warden side with Greg, a janitor, over you, a psychologist? The Warden is an idiot, not a complete moron."

"The relationship between father and son can be complicated."

"What are you saying? The Warden is Greg's dad?"

"I'm afraid so," he replied. "I believe Coffee will skew it, put all the blame on Greg and leave the Warden untouched and blameless, but you deserve to know the truth."

My stab wound throbbed. I had assumed the guards put up with Greg's antics and interruptions because of his boyish charm, but no, they were scared of Daddy Dearest. Blood drummed my temples. I'd kill for another Percocet—dizziness be damned.

"Greg admitted to everything: your ex's murder, Jonathan's attempted murder, coming here to kill him in front of you. It goes without saying that Greg has been decompensating for quite some time."

"Well, I don't give a shit if he's been attending Hogwarts for quite some time," I snapped. "He's a psychopath who *literally* picked me out of a crowd and ruined my life. None of your psychological bullshit can justify that!"

Dr. Sean shook his head emphatically. "There is no justification for what he's done. He violated your privacy, your freedom, and your trust. It's indefensible, and I'd never try to convince you otherwise."

"Okay," I said, winding down slightly. "Wait, there was someone else there. In Jonathan's room. In the bathroom."

He nodded. "There was."

"Who was it?"

"Jonathan's mother. She was in the bathroom when you came into the room, and she heard everything. She's the one who called the police." Dr. Sean let a smile slip. "Punched Greg pretty hard too, knocked him out."

"Ah, the in-laws."

"Look on the bright side; you skipped the awkward first meeting."

"Yeah." I chuckled, wincing as the stitches pulled. "What's awkward about mounting another man while her comatose son lies in the next bed?"

"She knows you did that to save Jonathan." Dr. Sean rubbed his head and sighed. "I know you've received therapy in the past, but this is an entirely new set of circumstances, and I'd highly recommend you receive additional counseling. Something trauma focused. If you could put your reluctance aside, I think you would benefit—"

"I'm all for it."

"You are?"

"Oh yeah, I'm a hot mess." I tapped my temple. "It's the Bay of Pigs up here."

He looked relieved. "I'll refer you to someone. Now, rest."

CHAPTER 63

It's a Blueberry Pancake Kind of Life

Two weeks after I stabbed myself, Jonathan woke up from his coma. It wasn't like the movies. Things weren't perfect. He had to learn to walk and talk again. I had expected the walking, but the talking was a shock. His speech was garbled; he mixed up words, or simply couldn't find them. Each and every day he worked with a speech pathologist, and some days were hard—really hard. He'd get frustrated with himself and with us, scared that he'd never get back to normal. And in some ways, things never would go back to normal, but after forty-five days, they were normal enough for him to be discharged.

A month after that, on a cool autumn morning, I went over to Jonathan's apartment and found him sleeping like an angel—one with horrible, morning dragon breath. Going back to school had been taxing; he needed to sleep. So being the considerate, loving girlfriend I was, I let him sleep.

For another three seconds.

"Goooood morning!" I bounced on his bed cheerily.

He groaned and pulled me into his morning warmth. "You're a monster."

I rested with my cheek against his heart. "Do you know what day it is?"

"Hm?" he grunted, slipping back into sleep.

"Greg's sentencing."

"Thank God." He opened one eye. "Do you want to be there for that?"

"Not even a little."

"In that case"—he morphed into a big spoon and I snuggled in—"you want pancakes?"

"YES! You think I came here just to see your lovely face?" I reached up, feeling around for his cheeks. I felt the three scars on his left one.[37] I squeezed both scarred and unscarred cheeks as he lazily swatted my hand away.

"You're the worst kind of morning person," he mumbled. "Blueberry pancakes?"

"Please."

His chest rose and fell against my back. "All right, just . . . give me a minute."

My life had changed rapidly since that day with Greg in the hospital. There was an official investigation of the Warden after Greg's indiscretions came to light. As it turned out, the Warden was not only guilty of nepotism, but was apparently grossly misappropriating funds (*cough* embezzlement *cough*). Therefore, the Warden was fired, and he was now facing charges of his own. What goes around comes around, buddy.

---

37 A little bubble of guilt still inflated in my chest when I thought about his scars. He was still handsome, but it didn't change the fact that he'd carry those scars forever. Thankfully, Jonathan thought they made him look badass and didn't complain about them.

Even better, the state expunged my record, and I landed a job at a reputable daycare. You know the kind, where corporate parents watch their kids through a webcam like zoo animals. And to top it all off, after my stab wound healed, I started going to an awesome therapist and burned the jewelry box that Greg gave me in an extremely liberating inferno. Life was a whirl-wind of courage, forgiveness, transformation, and restoration. All good things turned sideways, whisked together, whirled—shaken, but not stirred.

But there was a moment there that I was nervous every-thing was changing too quickly. I was afraid it would be too much to handle, that things were getting out of control. Then I happened to flip on the news, and staring back at me was none other than Nympho Yvette. As always, she was fiercely tiny and tatted, with a grin like a Bond villain. Her mug shot was side by side with that of a tall, dark, and handsome man, who the news anchor referred to as Francesco. Oh YES, DECAF FRANCES-CO. Apparently, she and Francesco were on the run after a four-way sex romp at a nursing home left an elderly couple dead, but (according to initial reports) satisfied. Anyone with information on their whereabouts was encouraged to call the tip line.

It was a much-needed reminder that life is messy and un-predictable, but among the chaos, there are beautiful constants: the rising and setting sun, the unbridled laughter of children, and Nympho Yvette's deadly hoo-ha.

It's a dichotomy that gives us hope; a dichotomy I intend-ed to celebrate with blueberry pancakes.

Epilogue

Greg was sentenced to spend the rest of his days at a specialty prison for men in northern Montana. The main "character building" program of the facility is custodial work for a treatment center for incontinent, lactose-intolerant children. According to sources, the kids sneak a lot of ice cream and yogurt.

I regularly send them a large cheese plate in thanks.

Acknowledgments

Thank you, Mom, for being my alpha reader and supporter, and for forgiving me for all the swear words that somehow slipped in there. And thank you, Dad, for sitting on the porch with me, helping me sort through the publishing world.

Shout out to Aric Weber (hey, sexy), Kim Lyons, Phil Lowry, Connie Shultz, and Kelly Dowling for being my beta readers (and not burning my manuscript in a massive inferno).

Thank you to the following amazing friends and family whom I bombarded with questions often via text (often at odd hours), and yet they didn't block my number: Ashley Young, Corey Wolff, Dave Wilcox, Rianna Wilcox, Heather Vlasuk, Justine Stewart, Cindy Sharrer, Heather Santone, McKenna Martone, Miranda MacKinnon, Hallie Lobaugh, Andrea Lau, Abby Kessler, Cassidy Higginbotham, Katie Heideman, Brenda Gregory, Judy Fronzaglia, Kim Creese, and Sharon Aikens. (That reverse alphabetical order is for you, Ash!)

Lastly, thank you to Katherine Miller (editor extraordinaire plus some)—this book would not have happened without you and your keen eye and your honest opinions and your insights and your ability to talk me off the ledge. THANK YOU.

Made in the USA
Middletown, DE
02 February 2018